The CAT EXPERT

Rebecca Watson

Project Consultant: Dr. D. G. Hessayon

Published by Expert Books
a division of Transworld Publishers

Copyright © Rebecca Watson and Dr. D. G. Hessayon 2010

The right of Rebecca Watson to be identified as author of this work
and Dr. D. G. Hessayon as Project Consultant for the work has been asserted
in accordance with sections 77 and 78 of the Copyright Designs and Patents Act 1988.

Illustrations copyright © Robin Watson 2010

A catalogue record for this book is available from the British Library

TRANSWORLD PUBLISHERS
61-63 Uxbridge Road, London W5 5SA
a division of the Random House Group Ltd

Distributed in the United States
by Sterling Publishing Co. Inc.,
387 Park Avenue South,
New York,
NY 10016-8810

EXPERT BOOKS

CONTENTS

Chapter 1 **WHO IS YOUR CAT?** 3–23

Chapter 2 **ALL ABOUT YOUR CAT** 24–43

Chapter 3 **KEEPING YOUR CAT HAPPY** 44–79

Chapter 4 **YOUR CAT'S HEALTH** 80–99

Chapter 5 **YOUR CAT'S BEHAVIOUR** 100–107

Chapter 6 **BREEDING FROM YOUR CAT** 108–113

Chapter 7 **SHOWING YOUR CAT** 114–118

Chapter 8 **YOUR CAT AND THE LAW** 119

Chapter 9 **FANTASTIC CATS** 120–125

Appendix **USEFUL CONTACTS** 126

INDEX 127–128

ACKNOWLEDGEMENTS 128

Designed by Robert Updegraff

Printed and bound by Butler Tanner & Dennis Ltd, Frome, Somerset

ISBN 978 09035056 8 0

© Rebecca Watson and Dr. D. G. Hessayon 2010

Chapter 1

WHO IS YOUR CAT?

Cats are relatively cheap and are not difficult to look after. They are proven stress-busters, make great pest controllers and are a wonderful addition to most households. For these and a hundred other reasons, cats are now the most popular pet in many countries across the world, including the UK and USA.

Every cat is unique: his* behaviour and appearance depend on any number of different factors, including his genes, his early experiences and the environment in which he lives. However, before we consider what you are looking for in your cat, it is important to think about you and your own circumstances.

The most common mistake that the potential cat owner makes is to believe that cats do not need much attention. This is not the case. If you are considering keeping one of these beautiful animals as a pet there are a number of questions you must ask yourself to make sure that a cat really is the best pet for you.

*The cat in the text throughout this book is referred to as 'he', but the words apply equally to female cats.

QUESTIONS ABOUT YOU

Can you provide a cat with a basic level of care?

This is the first and most important question you must ask yourself. Basic care includes:

- Fresh water and a balanced meat-based diet.
- Exercise and scratching facilities.
- A clean litter tray.
- Companionship and commitment.
- Identification, such as a microchip.
- Grooming.
- A sheltered and safe place to live.
- Veterinary attention, both routine and in emergencies.
- Someone to look after your cat when you are away.

If you think anything on this list is likely to cause you problems, then a cat is not the right pet for you. If you can offer these things, however, then congratulations – you are ready for a big adventure.

Can you afford a cat?

You should budget for around £50 per month for the average cat. That would cover your regular costs – food, insurance, litter, and flea and worm treatments. You should also consider the cost of:

- Neutering – a one-off cost of around £30–£50 for a male cat or £40–£70 for a female cat.
- Microchipping – a one-off cost of around £20–£30.
- Cat toys – £20 a year or more, depending on what you buy.
- Grooming equipment – a one-off cost of around £20 for a basic kit.
- Carriers – a one-off cost of around £20–£50.
- Bedding – a one-off cost of around £10–£50.
- Scratching posts – around £10–£20 per year, depending on the quality of the scratcher and how often your cat uses it.
- Catteries or petsitters – for a seven-day holiday, one cat would cost approximately £45–£50 to keep in a cattery, or around £55–£80 to be cared for by a petsitter.
- Emergency veterinary treatment – anything from £60 to £3,000 or more. Note that a good insurance policy should protect you from the cost of the more expensive treatments. Policies vary greatly depending on what kind of cover you want, but a monthly premium of between £10 and £20 is normal for one cat. For more information on insurance policies, see pages 98–99.

How much time can you spend with your cat?

Do you spend very little time at home? If so, you should think carefully about why you want a cat, what kind of cat will cope best on his own and how you will provide for him when you are not there.

Cats do tend to be more independent than dogs, but some, due to their character, age or health, will require more time from you. You may want to consider two cats so that they have companionship while you are away, but don't forget to double the costs.

Where do you live?

Think about what kind of cat would suit your living arrangements. Do you live in a flat with no garden or on a farm? In a high-rise flat or a detached house? In the suburbs or a city centre? Check your rental or lease agreement to see if you are allowed pets in your property. If you are not, don't get one.

The indoors–outdoors debate

Can a cat be happy living permanently indoors with no access to the outside world? This is something that most people – prospective owners, vets and breeders alike – cannot agree on. Despite the arguments, very few cats would elect to remain indoors if they were given the choice. So, if possible, you should always provide some sort of outdoor access, even if it is enclosed. However, every cat is different and where a situation may suit one it may be totally inappropriate for another. You may find that individual rehoming centres or breeders have a preference for either indoors or outdoors, or that some cats cannot go outside for health reasons. For more information on the arguments for and against keeping your cat indoors, and on keeping your cat safe inside and out, see pages 49–55.

Do you have other pets?

When they work, multi-pet households are very rewarding, but when animals don't have enough space or aren't introduced properly, issues can manifest themselves in behaviour problems. If you have dogs or other cats, introductions to the new cat will have to be carefully managed to make sure no problems arise – see pages 47–48 for more on introducing a new cat successfully.

Making introductions will be more demanding if you have a dog that chases cats, a territorial pet that won't accept intruders or a sensitive pet who may find the addition of another animal stressful. Carefully choosing the age, sex and character of your new cat to complement your other pet or pets will help. Also, don't forget any rodents, reptiles, fish or birds you have. How will they cope when one of the world's top predators moves in?

Who else lives in your family home?

Do the other members of the household like cats? Are there young children in the house who need to be taught how to treat a cat? Is it a busy house with people coming and going all the time?

Many cats are bought and then rehomed a few months later because someone in the home has an allergy. Find out before you get a cat whether anyone is severely allergic by visiting a cat adoption centre or breeder. If someone is moderately allergic and you all still want a cat, there are things you can do that will help – see page 97 for more information.

Can you live with your cat's natural behaviour?

The following are natural behaviours and you should be prepared to live with them if you want a cat:

- Scratching – both outside and inside.
- Hunting – some cats catch and bring prey into the house, dead or alive!
- Moulting and hairballs – your cat will moult, leaving hair on your floors, furniture and clothes for much of the time. Your house and clothes will require regular vacuuming and brushing if you want to keep the cat hair under control, particularly in the heavier moulting seasons. Your cat may also throw up hairballs.
- Territorial and sexual behaviour – if you do not neuter your cat, it is likely that he or she will fight, spray or caterwaul as part of territorial or sexual behaviour.

What are your future plans?

No one expects you to be able to tell the future, but owning a cat is a long-term responsibility. You may be thinking of moving abroad or planning to have children – are you able to stick by your cat through these times? Cats live to an average age of 16, but some live to 20 or more. If you're not willing to commit to this length of time, then you should think twice about a cat, or perhaps consider rehoming an older cat.

What will your cat give you?

You may want a cat for companionship, or as a family pet, for showing or breeding, or as a working cat (to catch mice or rats), or for any number of other reasons. You may want a calm, adult moggy, an energetic, pedigree kitten, or even a problem cat to rehabilitate. Whatever you are looking for, pages 6–21 will help you decide on the kind of cat that is best for you.

5

QUESTIONS ABOUT YOUR CAT

What kind of character are you looking for?

Cats are not just independent and aloof. They can be noisy, needy, attention seeking, funny or mischievous. The following are only examples of basic character types – each cat is different and most owners come to love their cat's unique personality.

THE INDEPENDENT CAT

Also known as a 'latchkey cat', he comes and goes as he pleases and spends lots of time outside. He enjoys human company but is not keen on very close contact. He is happy to be left alone and won't pine for human companions. Note that an independent cat is not to be confused with a 'feral cat' – see page 49.

    The independent cat makes a good pet, particularly if you are out during the day. Very young children may bother him but a confident independent cat would happily live with a friendly dog.

THE LAP CAT

The lap cat is a homebody. He goes outside once in a while but will soon be back inside. He waits for his human companions to return home and likes their company. Lap cats are ideal companions and family pets. They may be happiest if their owners are often at home, but might be just as content with a dog or another cat for company.

THE DEPENDENT CAT

The dependent cat follows his human family around and miaows when they are out of sight. He sits on their laps at every opportunity and only really likes going outside with them. He pines when they are away from home.

    Dependent cats make very good companions and thrive in situations where there are always people around. Someone who rarely leaves home and constantly gives their cat attention may find that the cat develops a dependent character. Although mostly harmless, this kind of behaviour can become a problem if a cat becomes over-dependent – see 'Behaviour Problems', page 101.

JUDGING YOUR CAT'S CHARACTER

Your new cat's personality will be affected by many things: inherited traits, his early experiences with his mother, his litter mates and humans, and his environment.

    If personality is important to you, you will have most success if you rehome an adult cat because the person caring for him will usually be able to tell you about the cat's past life, his behaviour, his likes and dislikes.

    If you buy a kitten, the adult cat you end up with will be partly down to luck. There might be signs that suggest your kitten is going to grow up to be active or lazy, playful or serious, outgoing or shy, but he is still learning so his personality is still being formed. For more on the advantages and disadvantages of age, see page 7.

Inherited traits

When you go to buy your kitten, watch how the mother reacts to the different kittens, and how they react to each other and to you. For example, the kitten who is first to investigate new things is likely to be confident. His brother, who waits until the new object has been sniffed at and pawed by the rest of the litter before daring to approach, will be more shy. The kitten who launches into play with his litter mates will probably grow up to enjoy chasing, playing and hunting. The kitten who sits quietly when you pick him up will almost certainly enjoy sitting on your lap when he is older. His sister who wriggles to get away may be more independent and may not enjoy close contact.

Early experience

The first eight weeks of a kitten's life are the most important time in his development. A kitten who does not come across household noises, human handling or dogs during these crucial weeks will find it difficult to accept them later.

Environment

Although the first eight weeks are vital, even the most confident and outgoing adult cat will start to avoid children or dogs if he learns that they are likely to chase or hurt him. Careful introductions to family life and a comforting environment will help your cat remain confident and happy. See Chapter 3 for more information on how to introduce your new kitten or cat successfully and how to keep him happy.

BREED CHARACTERISTICS

Some breeds show certain characteristics. For example, the Siamese is generally much more active and noisy than the Persian, which is more often a quiet lap cat. You can never guarantee that your kitten will grow up to be a typical example of his breed, but it's a good place to start. See pages 15–21 for more on pedigree and non-pedigree cats.

Mousers

The world's most successful known mouser was Towser, who was employed by the Glenturret Distillery in Tayside, Scotland, to protect the barley. Over almost 24 years' service she caught nearly 29,000 rodents. Her replacement, Amber, didn't catch one. Which just goes to show, you never can tell what you are going to get!

What age would you like your cat to be?

There is a big difference between kittens and adult cats. They may be cute, but kittens are hard work, and will need special attention for their first year of life. Think carefully about your own life and plans before you decide whether a kitten or an adult cat is right for you.

KITTENS – CUTE, BUT HARD WORK

Advantages

- You can watch your pet mature and change throughout his life.
- You can help develop his character by the way you treat him, and you will know his history should any problems arise in later life.
- Other pets more easily accept a new kitten because they feel less threatened by such a young addition to the household.

Disadvantages

- A young cat, like a child, will need close supervision. He will need feeding more often than an adult cat, he will be noisier at night, may need litter training, and is more likely to want to scratch or destroy things.
- Although they seem less threatening when small, you may find that an adolescent cat quickly becomes dominant in a house with elderly cats or dogs about.
- It is more difficult to tell what sort of character your kitten will grow up to have.

ADULTS – NOT SO YOUNG, NOT SO MUCH TROUBLE

Advantages

- Older often means wiser and quieter. Adult cats do not need supervision, will usually sit more quietly on your lap, and can be left at home alone while you work.
- Rehoming an adult cat means you can find out who he is before taking him home. Does he use a litter tray or does he go outside to the toilet? Does he get on with dogs? With children? Does he scratch? Will he let you groom him?
- An adult cat will probably have been neutered and microchipped already, so you will not need to pay for these things.

Disadvantages

- An adult cat can be harder to introduce into your home. He may not have lived with children or other cats or dogs before, or he may have been used to better access to the outside than you are able to provide.
- If you rehome a very old cat, you will have to be prepared to cope with losing him, possibly after only a few years.

7

Do you want a male or female cat?

If you have no other cats or dogs and your new cat has been neutered, it does not matter what sex you choose. However, if you do not plan to neuter your new cat, or if you already have a cat or dog, then the sex of your new cat is important as it will make a big difference to his or her behaviour.

SHOULD I NEUTER MY CAT?

An un-neutered tom (male cat) will display strong territorial and sexual behaviour. This will include aggression and fighting, straying long distances in search of a mate and spraying urine to mark his territory.

An un-neutered queen (female cat) will attract toms to your house, and will wail or caterwaul when she is ready to mate. If she is not kept away from male cats she will regularly have litters of kittens and is likely to get injuries from mating.

Neutering is the removal of the sexual organs to stop unplanned births and avoid unwanted sexual and territorial behaviour. Apart from a very small risk associated with the general anaesthetic needed for the operation, there are no other disadvantages to neutering, and a neutered cat is the mark of a caring and responsible owner.

In most cases, breeders of pedigree cats and rehoming organizations will only let you have a kitten if you neuter him or her. Any adult cat you rehome from an organization will almost certainly have been neutered already. For more information on neutering see page 81.

KEEPING UN-NEUTERED PETS

All un-neutered animals display territorial and sexual behaviour towards other animals, who are seen as either enemies or potential mates. Keeping two un-neutered animals together (e.g. a cat and a dog), even of the same sex, may well cause mayhem and is not a good idea.

If you want to breed from cats and you want to keep both sexes, you will need enough room in your house to keep them separated while also giving them a good quality of life. They should not be allowed to go outside unless you have an escape-proof cat run in your garden.

OPPOSITES ATTRACT

Although no guarantee can be given, getting a neutered cat of the opposite sex to your other neutered pets will increase your chances of successfully integrating them. Just as an older cat feels less threatened by a kitten, a male cat or dog is less likely to have confrontations with a small female cat than with a large male and vice versa. If you are getting two kittens at the same time and you plan to neuter them both, their sex is less likely to matter because they will grow up together. Nevertheless, problems do still occasionally occur as they reach adulthood.

If both are neutered and carefully introduced, it is possible for cats and house rabbits to be friends, but they should be supervised at all times.

What would you like your cat to look like?

Although not nearly as varied as dogs, cats are surprisingly different in size, shape and colour. A cat's appearance doesn't greatly affect his behaviour, but it may give you clues about the kind of care he will need.

YOUR CAT'S BODY SHAPE

It is true that dogs come in a wider variety of shapes and sizes than cats, but compare a Persian, a Sphynx and a Maine Coon side by side and you will see as many differences as you will find similarities.

Cats are described as having one of two basic body shapes, 'cobby' or 'foreign', and can range from being 'extreme cobby' to 'extreme foreign'. Most cats are somewhere in the middle, and are said to be 'moderate' in shape.

Cobby

This body shape is common in breeds that have evolved in colder climates because their thickset bodies retain heat. An 'extreme cobby' type would be the Persian.

Foreign

This body shape is common in breeds that have evolved in warmer climates because their thin bodies help to shed heat. An 'extreme foreign' type would be the Oriental Shorthair.

The changing shape of cats

So far, changes to the appearance of the cat have been small, such as different fur types and colours. However, in recent years we have seen an increase in cross-breeding domestic with wild cats, and new breeds created from one individual born with a random genetic deformity. Reproducing cats like this often requires intensive inbreeding programmes, where a male offspring is bred back to his mother.

Perhaps the most dramatic changes over the last 20 or 30 years have been in the head shapes of two very old breeds, the Siamese and the Persian. The Siamese used to have a much softer outline but now the standard shows an extremely angular shape, while many Persians were bred with virtually no muzzle. Thankfully much of this latter practice has stopped now because of the serious health implications, including constricted tearducts and breathing problems.

A recent addition to the cat family, the Munchkin, has been bred to have very short legs, much like a Dachshund. Controversial because of its unnatural shape, the breed is not recognized for showing in the UK.

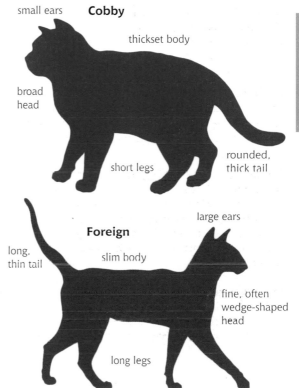

Cobby

small ears · thickset body · broad head · short legs · rounded, thick tail

Foreign

large ears · long, thin tail · slim body · fine, often wedge-shaped head · long legs

The Toyger is an example of a new coloration: it is essentially a tabby cat but bred to have the distinctive tiger stripe. Further selective breeding is planned to widen the face and bridge of the nose and to round the ears so that a more tiger-like look is gained.

The Munchkin.

The Toyger's tiger-like colouring makes it an increasingly popular new breed of pedigree cat.

9

YOUR CAT'S COAT

Longhaired, dense coats are beautiful, soft and lovely to stroke, but they take time to look after. Hairless or curly-coated cats are unusual but also require special care. Fine, short coats are the most common and the easiest to care for. All cats moult (shed their fur) throughout the year.

Cats are usually shorthaired or longhaired. It is commonly believed that longhaired cats are more docile than their shorthaired counterparts but this is not always the case. Fur length mainly affects the way a cat looks and the amount of grooming he needs.

Shorthaired cats

The majority of cats are shorthaired. They need very little grooming as long as they are able to do it themselves. A quick comb once a fortnight is usually sufficient for very fine, shorthaired coats, but denser fur may need a bit more attention.

The long, luxurious coat of the Persian makes it a very stunning cat, but does require dedicated daily combing to prevent mats.

The Siamese has a short and fine coat, making it very easy to care for.

The Turkish Angora is sometimes referred to as a semi-longhair because of its finer longhaired coat.

Longhaired cats

Traditional longhaired cats, such as Persians, need daily grooming to stop their fur becoming matted and dirty, which can lead to skin disease and pain. You should only consider a breed with a coat like this if you have enough time to groom him every day.

Many longhaired cats, like the Oriental Longhair, are referred to as **semi-longhaired**. This term describes cats that have very fine, flat, longhaired coats. They do not need as much grooming as traditional longhairs.

The very dense but short coat of the British Shorthair is easy to care for but it may require a little more attention than a Siamese.

THE TEXTURE OF YOUR CAT'S FUR

The texture of your cat's coat is determined by the number and proportion of the different types of hairs that make up his fur – see pages 28–29 for more information on the types of hairs.

Straight-coated cats

The vast majority of cats have fur that is straight. It can be fine or dense, and either rough or smooth. The different types of hairs in a cat's coat are soft, smooth or rough and the texture of the coat depends on the proportions of these in his fur.

Some cats, like the British Shorthair and Chartreux, have fur that appears to stand up from the body. This is called a double coat and it is like this because these cats have a lot of hairs all of the same length, making their coats very thick.

Hairless cats and curly coats

Hairless and curly-coated cats are the result of genetic accidents. Although any kitten can be born naturally hairless or curly, a few pedigree types have been specially bred like this. If you are thinking of getting a cat with an unusual coat, it is vital that you research the individual grooming needs and possible problems of the breed.

Although it appears entirely bald, the Sphynx is in fact covered in a soft, downy fur.

Hairless cats, like the Sphynx, only look hairless. They do in fact have down hairs, the softest, finest type, but lack awn and guard hairs. Strangely, hairless cats need regular grooming because of the oils that build up on their skin. They are very vulnerable to sunburn and cold and are mostly kept as indoor cats for this reason.

Curly-coated cats, like the Devon Rex, are quite easy to groom but some have almost no fur in places. So, like hairless cats, they get a build-up of oil on the skin. They are also vulnerable to the outside elements.

This Siamese–Devon Rex crossbreed shows the classic curled fur of Rex breeds.

COAT COLOURS

Cats come in all sorts of colours and patterns. Some people believe that certain colours or patterns affect character but this is unlikely. The pattern and colour of a kitten can alter very slightly over the first year of his life. You are unlikely to be able to judge your kitten's final colour from looking at the parent cats, because quite often the parents are a completely different colour and pattern from their offspring.

Cats can have just one colour in their coat or many colours. The 'original' domestic cat is thought to have been a tabby. In the wild, this was an effective camouflage and made tabby cats very successful hunters. For this reason, pure, solid-coloured coats (called 'selfs') are less common, although selective breeding has now developed these in many different shades. There are full, deep colours and diluted, pale colours, and, just to make things confusing, breeders often use different names for the same colour, such as ginger, red or auburn.

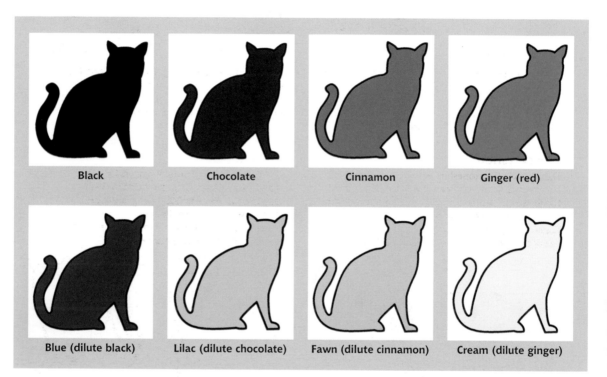

| Black | Chocolate | Cinnamon | Ginger (red) |
| Blue (dilute black) | Lilac (dilute chocolate) | Fawn (dilute cinnamon) | Cream (dilute ginger) |

Hair colour

The individual hairs in a cat's coat can also be patterned with different colours, which adds to the beauty and depth of the fur. There are five variations, each of which gives a distinctive appearance:

Self
A single-colour cat with no variation in the individual hairs is called a solid- or self-coloured cat.

Tipped
Tipped hairs have a small tip of colour at the end of the guard or awn hairs. Cats with this colouring appear to have very light swirls of colour on a mainly solid coat.

Shaded
Shaded hairs have a much deeper-coloured tip at the end of the guard or awn hairs. Cats with this colouring appear to have dark swirls of colour on a pale background. If the coat is parted, the pale downy undercoat should be clearly visible.

Smoke
Smoke hairs have only a very short pale base. If the cat is still it can be hard to tell the difference between this and a 'self' coat, but as the cat moves the light undercoat is clearly contrasted with the darker tips.

Ticked
Ticking is thought to be the 'original' fur colouring of the domestic cat. Each hair alternates between dark and light in bands of colour which help give the cat excellent camouflage.

COAT PATTERNS

Cats come in a dizzying array of different pattern variations.

Tabby

This is the most common pattern found in cats. There are many different variations, most often defined by dark stripes or patches with a ticked background.

Classic (or blotched). Dark-coloured stripes of varying widths that form a swirling pattern on the body, with a ringed tail.

Mackerel (or striped). Thin dark stripes running down the sides of the body, a ringed tail and often a dark stripe down the spine.

Spotted. Dark stripes broken into smaller patches. The full stripes often remain on the tail and legs.

Ticked. Speckled fur covering the whole body, with almost no clear dark patches.

Tortoiseshell

The traditional tortoiseshell pattern is made up of equal amounts of black and red and is often called **tortie**. Some cats have a tortoiseshell pattern in the dilute colours of cream and blue.

Tortie tabby. Both tabby and tortoiseshell patterns can occur together on one cat, called a **torbie**.

Bi-coloured

This is a coat made up of white and another colour. The other colour can be solid, such as ginger, or a pattern, such as ginger tabby. Tortoiseshell and white bi-colour (occasionally called **tri-colour**) cats are sometimes known as **calico** cats.

Tortoiseshell **Tortoiseshell and white** **Bi-coloured tabby** **Ginger and white bi-coloured**

Tuxedo

Some black-and-white bi-colour cats are referred to as tuxedo cats, because their colouring makes them look as though they are wearing a tuxedo.

Pointed (or colourpoint)

When a cat's ears, face, paws and tail are a darker colour than the body, it is known as 'pointed'. This is most often seen in the Siamese breed. A cat can also be pointed with a pattern, such as tabby or tortie.

Your kitten's coat may change

Patterns are often visible from a very young age, but there can be some slight alteration in colour and pattern over the first year of a kitten's life. Solid-coloured kittens sometimes have 'ghost' tabby markings in their fur at first but lose them later. Kittens with light colouring, particularly those which are pointed or have tipped hairs, are often late to develop their full adult colour. White kittens may show a few black hairs at first but will usually lose these later. Tabby kittens show their markings clearly from birth but they, and most other kittens, usually develop deeper colours over their first year.

13

EYE COLOUR

Kittens are all born with blue eyes, which then develop over time into their true colour. Adult cats' eyes are green, brown, yellow or blue, and can be a whole range of different shades.

This kitten has blue eyes now but these will probably change to a different colour as he grows up.

Blue-eyed white cats and deafness

The genetic defect that causes deafness is linked to the genes for white fur and blue eyes. Although not all white cats with blue eyes are deaf, most deaf cats are white with blue eyes! A white cat may also have one blue eye and one yellow eye. These cats are often deaf in the ear on the blue-eyed side but hear perfectly well in the other.

This odd-eyed cat is deaf in his right ear but can hear in his left.

Colour and its link with sex

Certain colours are more common in either males or females. For example, two out of three ginger cats are male (hence the well-known image of the 'ginger tom'). However, if you want a tortoiseshell cat, your odds of finding a male drop dramatically. Only one tortie cat in every 40,000 is a male, making tortoiseshell the most gender-related pattern.

Why most ginger cats are male

Male cats carry an X- and a Y-chromosome, while females carry two X-chromosomes. The colour ginger is carried only on the X-chromosome and is dominant over all other colours – i.e. if one parent cat is ginger and the other brown or black, the ginger will dominate and the male offspring, with only one X-chromosome, will be ginger. Because a female has a second X-chromosome she can inherit another colour as well as ginger, in which case some of her cells will follow the ginger X-chromosome and the rest the other colour, making her, for example, ginger and brown or ginger and black (tortoiseshell). For a female to be completely ginger she must have two ginger X-chromosomes, then no matter which one her cells follow, her hair will be ginger.

Why most tortoiseshell cats are female

Tortoiseshell is a combination of two colours (ginger and black). Each of these is passed down only on an X-chromosome, so a cat needs two X-chromosomes (i.e. female) to be tortoiseshell. Male tortoiseshells do exist, but they are the result of a genetic mutation or the fusion of the two colours in the womb.

Would you like a pedigree or a non-pedigree cat?

The key differences between a pedigree and non-pedigree cat are price and choice.

WHY CHOOSE NON-PEDIGREE?

Non-pedigree cats are also known as moggies, mixed-breeds or crossbreeds (a term particularly used for a mixture of two different pedigrees). Moggies are more robust than pedigree cats: they have inherited the best qualities from a long, varied gene pool. They are less likely to suffer from the inherited genetic defects and health problems of pedigree cats. Non-pedigree cats and kittens are very common, so you will have lots of choice. They come in any colour, shape and size and usually cost around £40–£60.

WHY CHOOSE PEDIGREE?

There are over 60 different pedigree breeds, specially bred to show particular genetic traits that will score points in the show ring. They are bred to quite specific colours, shapes and sizes, so if you want a particular 'look', then you should be able to find a cat to match your requirements. Some breeds are associated with certain character traits too – for example, if you are looking for a noisy cat a Siamese would be a good bet, or if you want a calm cat a Persian might suit you. See the following pages for more information about breeds.

Pedigree cats are not as common as moggies, so if you are looking for a specific breed you may have to travel quite far, in some cases abroad, to get one. When a pedigree cat has a litter, it is only the kittens regarded as unsuitable for showing or breeding that are sold on as family pets, so you may not get a large choice and you often have to go on a waiting list. If you want a show-quality cat, be prepared to pay more. Pedigree cats cost much more than non-pedigrees – anything from £300 to £10,000. They also cost more to insure and are desirable to thieves.

Do your research

If you do plan to get a pedigree cat, you should research carefully to find out what it is like to live with a particular breed. To get you started, a list of breeds with some essential notes follows. However, please bear in mind:

- The kitten you get may not conform to his breed type.
- Breeds that are particularly unsuited to indoor-only living are highlighted but *all* cats appreciate some access to the outside world.
- Health problems mentioned here are gathered from worldwide reports. Your cat will not necessarily develop the disorders associated with his breed.

Non-pedigree and pedigree colouring

Non-pedigree cats come in all patterns and colours but pedigree breeds are bred to look a certain way. The longer selective breeding continues, the more often new colour and pattern combinations occur. For example, all Siamese cats once had a cream body with dark seal-brown points; with selective breeding, however, the Siamese today comes in a huge array of colours and patterns.

A huge variety of pedigree cats is available, but they do come at a cost.

Non-pedigrees make wonderful family pets and are very easy to find.

GUIDE TO BREEDS

Key to symbols

Grooming

🛁	infrequent, easy
🛁🛁	regular, moderate
🛁🛁🛁	frequent, difficult

Breed stereotype

●	easygoing
●●	moderate
●●●	demanding

🛋	affectionate lap cat
🐈	likes company
🐈	independent

✹	likes outdoor access
👫	good with all ages
🎵	vocal

Who is your cat?

Longhaired cats

AMERICAN CURL

Physical description: Medium, cobby with ears that curl backwards. Medium-length, fine fur. All colours and patterns.
Character: Gentle, active and affectionate.
Grooming: 🛁🛁🛁
Breed stereotype: ●● 🛋 ✹
Health: Susceptible to ear complaints.
Notes: This breed is not recognized by all breeding and showing councils because they object to the intentional breeding of a genetic deformity. There is also a shorthaired variety.

BALINESE*

Physical description: Medium and foreign with a plume tail and medium-length fine fur. Always pointed with solid colour, tabby or tortie patterns. Usually in lilac, blue, chocolate or seal. Blue eyes.
Character: Active, intelligent and vocal.
Grooming: 🛁🛁
Breed stereotype: ●●● 🐈 🎵
Health: Reported gum problems and heart disease.
Notes: These cats are longhaired Siamese. Some varieties are referred to as Javanese in the US.

BIRMAN**

Physical description: Medium and moderate with fine, silky fur. Pale with darker points, white paws and blue eyes.
Character: Gentle, quiet and intelligent.
Grooming: 🛁🛁
Breed stereotype: ● 🛋 🐈 👫
Health: Reported blood, kidney and nervous system disorders.
Notes: Also known as the Sacred Cat of Burma.

CYMRIC See Manx.

MAINE COON**

Physical description: Large and moderate with a heavy, shaggy and water-resistant coat, often with a neck ruff and bushy tail. Traditionally tabby; other colours and patterns available but not chocolate, lilac or pointed.
Character: Playful, active and adventurous.
Grooming: 🛁🛁
Breed stereotype: ●● 🐈 ✹
Health: Reported heart, gum and joint problems.
Notes: Makes a chirping noise instead of miaowing and tends to sleep in odd places. It is not true that this breed is either part wild cat or part racoon.

NEBELUNG See Russian Blue.

NORWEGIAN FOREST CAT**

Physical description: Large and moderate with dense, coarse and water-resistant coat, a neck ruff and very long tail. Most colours and patterns but not pointed, lilac or chocolate.
Character: Playful, active and adventurous.
Grooming: 🛁🛁🛁
Breed stereotype: ● 🐈 ✹
Health: Reported metabolism disorder.
Notes: A famous tree-climber, who comes down head first. Often appears in Scandinavian fairytales and legends.

ORIENTAL LONGHAIR*

Physical description: Medium and extreme foreign with medium-length fur and a plume tail. All patterns and colours but not pointed. Green eyes except for white varieties, which have blue eyes.
Character: Playful, intelligent and vocal.
Grooming: 🛁🛁
Breed stereotype: ●●● 🐈 🎵
Health: Reported liver disease and digestion problems.
Notes: Closely related to the Siamese. Was originally called the Angora in the UK but was changed to avoid confusion with the Turkish Angora. In some countries the name Javanese has been given to Oriental Longhairs.

** widely available in UK; * some availability in UK; others rare in UK. For definition of terms, see pages 9–13.

PERSIAN**

Physical description:
Medium and extreme cobby. Short-nosed with very dense, silky fur. All colours and patterns.
Character: Friendly, easygoing and inactive.
Grooming:
Breed stereotype:

Health: Some jaw, eye and breathing problems associated with the extreme short nose. Reports of gum disease and inherited kidney disease.
Notes: Other names used for describing varieties of this breed are Chinchilla, Longhair and Himalayan.

RAGDOLL**

Physical description: Large and cobby with dense, silky fur. Pointed, bi-colour or mitted (white-pawed) patterns with blue eyes. Pale base with seal, lilac, chocolate or blue patches of colour.
Character: Gentle, inactive and loyal.
Grooming: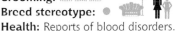
Breed stereotype:
Health: Reports of blood disorders.
Notes: An old wives' tale says that these cats cannot feel pain, but this is absolutely untrue.

SIBERIAN

Physical description: Large and cobby with dense, water-resistant coat and a neck ruff. Tabby is the most common pattern; all colours occur.
Character: Gentle, active and loyal.
Grooming:
Breed stereotype:
Health: No specific reported problems.
Notes: An old, naturally occurring breed.

SOMALI*

Physical description: Medium and foreign with a bushy tail and dense, medium-length fur that is always ticked. Red, blue or fawn with dark

outlines around the eyes and a tabby 'M' on the forehead.
Character: Energetic, bold and intelligent.
Grooming:
Breed stereotype: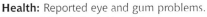
Health: Reported eye and gum problems.
Notes: A longhaired Abyssinian.

TIFFANY/CHANTILLY

Physical description: Medium and moderate with fine fur. Chocolate is the most common colour; can be solid or tabby.
Character: Gentle, inquisitive and playful.
Grooming:
Breed stereotype:
Health: No specific reported problems.
Notes: Often confused with the Tiffanie, which is a longhaired variety of the Burmilla.

TURKISH ANGORA

Physical description: Small to medium and moderate with silky, medium-length fur and a bushy tail. Traditionally white; other colours available but no points, chocolate or cinnamon.
Character: Outgoing, intelligent and athletic.
Grooming:
Breed stereotype:
Health: No specific reported problems.
Notes: A very old breed rescued from serious decline by a breeding programme in Turkey. Not to be confused with the Angora (the original name for the Oriental Longhair).

TURKISH VAN*

Physical description: Large and moderate with silky fur and a longer neck ruff and tail. Always chalk white with coloured patches (traditionally ginger) on tail and at base of ears. Yellow or odd-coloured eyes.
Character: Friendly, intelligent and active.
Grooming:
Breed stereotype:
Health: Some white-associated deafness.
Notes: Loves water. Sometimes called the Turkish Swimming Cat.

Shorthaired cats

ABYSSINIAN*

Physical description: Medium and foreign with short, smooth fur and dark lines around the eyes. Always ticked (agouti) in a variety of colours but traditionally a ruddy brown.

Character: Loyal, inquisitive and active.

Grooming:

Breed stereotype:

Health: Reports of kidney, gum and eye disorders.

Notes: Speculation surrounds the origin of the breed, but it is thought to be one of the oldest in existence. Bears a striking similarity to the cats painted by the Egyptians.

AMERICAN BOBTAIL

Physical description: Medium to large and cobby with a very short tail. Medium-length, shaggy fur with a ruff around the neck and longer hair on the hind legs. There is also a longhaired variety. Brown or grey tabby is most common.

Character: Intelligent, playful and sociable.

Grooming:

Breed stereotype:

Health: Skeletal defects.

Notes: Rare outside the US.

AMERICAN SHORTHAIR

Physical description: Large and extreme cobby with dense, stiff fur in all patterns and colours.

Character: Affectionate, calm and active.

Grooming:

Breed stereotype:

Health: No specific reported problems.

Notes: Bred originally from alley cats, the American Shorthair is still rare outside the US.

AMERICAN WIREHAIR

Physical description: Large and cobby with a round head. Dense, coarse, crimped coat. All colours and patterns.

Character: Active, affectionate and inquisitive.

Grooming:

Breed stereotype:

Health: No specific reported problems.

Notes: The first American Wirehair was born on a farm in the US in 1966. They are still rare outside the US.

BENGAL**

Physical description: Medium to large and moderate. Short, thick fur in spotted or classic tabby patterns with a black-tipped tail.

Character: Assertive, active and playful.

Grooming:

Breed stereotype:

Health: No specific reported problems.

Notes: The Bengal is the product of breeding the wild Asian Leopard Cat with a domestic cat. Early generations retained many of their wild instincts and did not make good pets. Selective breeding has made them much tamer.

BOMBAY

Physical description: Medium and cobby. Very short, smooth fur in solid black; coppery eyes.

Character: Friendly, curious and active.

Grooming:

Breed stereotype:

Health: Skull defects associated with the American Bombay.

Notes: Known as the mini-Panther, this breed is closely associated with the Burmese. In the US the Bombay is a breed but in the UK it is a variety of the Asian Group, along with the Tiffanie and Burmilla.

BRITISH SHORTHAIR**

Physical description: Large, extreme cobby with a round, large head. Double-layered, short and very dense fur sticks out from the body. All patterns and colours.

Character: Placid, friendly and inactive.

Grooming:

Breed stereotype:

Health: Reported blood disorder.

Notes: Lewis Carroll's Cheshire Cat was based on a British Shorthair.

BURMESE (AMERICAN AND EUROPEAN)**

Physical description: Medium. The American is cobby with a short nose whereas the European is more foreign in appearance. Smooth, short, satin coat usually in a dark brown, but torties and other colours are available.

Character: Demanding, lively and affectionate.
Grooming: 🏛
Breed stereotype: ● ● ● 🐈 🏠 ♫
Health: Skull defects associated with the American Burmese. Heart, eye and respiratory disorders. Diabetes.
Notes: This Burmese breed was founded by a cat called Wong Mau.

BURMILLA**

Physical description: Medium and moderate. Short, soft and dense coat in a tipped or shaded pattern with tabby stripes on the forehead, legs and tail. The original colour was lilac with green eyes but others have been developed.
Character: Relaxed, sociable and playful.
Grooming: 🏛
Breed stereotype: ● ● 🐈 🏠 👤 👥
Health: Kidney disorders associated with Persian breeding.
Notes: The Burmilla began with a Burmese x Persian Chinchilla breeding. There is a longhaired variety called a Tiffanie, not to be confused with the Tiffany/Chantilly.

CHARTREUX

Physical description: Large and cobby with a medium-length, woolly, water-resistant coat. Always blue with silver tipping and copper or orange eyes.
Character: Quiet, easygoing and sensitive.
Grooming: 🏛 🏛
Breed stereotype: ● ✹ 👤 👥
Health: Reported knee disorders.
Notes: A very old breed that originated in France. A peaceful cat that barely makes a sound and often looks as though it is smiling.

CORNISH REX

Physical description: Small to medium and foreign. Coat is curly, dense and very soft. All colours and patterns.
Character: Playful, affectionate and adventurous.
Grooming: 🏛 🏛
Breed stereotype:
● ● ● 🛋 🐈
Health: No specific reported problems.
Notes: This breed is often kept entirely or primarily indoors because it is very sensitive to the cold and wet. They should only ever go outside under close supervision and never in extreme temperatures. It is genetically different to the Devon Rex.

DEVON REX

Physical description: Medium and moderate/foreign with a very wedge-shaped face. Coat is wavy and sparse (particularly on the undercarriage). All colours and patterns.
Character: Active, playful and loyal.
Grooming: 🏛 🏛
Breed stereotype: ● ● ● 🛋 🐈
Health: Reports of joint, blood, skin and muscular disorders.
Notes: These cats are very sensitive to the cold and so are often kept entirely or primarily indoors. They should only ever go outside under close supervision and never in extreme temperatures.

EGYPTIAN MAU

Physical description: Medium and moderate with a dense, silky coat. There are different black and brown colour varieties, all based around shaded, ticked and spotted tabby patterns.
Character: Active, devoted and playful.
Grooming: 🏛
Breed stereotype: ● ● 🛋 🐈
Health: Reported heart and respiratory disorders.
Notes: This breed was originally brought to the US from Egypt by an exiled Russian princess. It is the only naturally occurring spotted breed.

EXOTIC SHORTHAIR**

Physical description: Medium and extreme cobby with dense, medium-length, plush fur that sticks out from the body. All colours and patterns.
Character: Placid, playful and affectionate.
Grooming: 🏛 🏛
Breed stereotype: ● 🛋 👤 👥
Health: Some respiratory, jaw and eye problems associated with the extreme short nose. Reports of inherited kidney disease.
Notes: This is a shorthaired, more active variety of the Persian.

JAPANESE BOBTAIL

Physical description: Small to medium and moderate with a very short tail. Soft, silky fur with little undercoat that forms a pompom on the tail. There is also a longhaired variety. Red, black or tortie-and-white bi- or tri-colours are most common.
Character: Sociable, inquisitive and active.
Grooming: 🏛
Breed stereotype: ● ● ✹ ♫
Health: No specific reported problems.
Notes: The Japanese good-luck charm, the Maneki Neko, is a Bobtail cat. This breed is entirely separate from the Manx.

KORAT*

Physical description: Small to medium, moderate with large eyes. Short, silky, single-layer fur, always blue (silver-tipped) with green eyes.
Character: Faithful, active and alert.
Grooming: 🏠
Breed stereotype: ● ● 🛋️ 🐱
Health: Reports of inherited muscular disorder.
Notes: Known as the 'good luck cat' in their native Thailand and sometimes given as wedding presents.

LAPERM

Physical description: Medium and foreign. Dense, tightly curled fur in both short- and longhaired varieties. A wide range of colours and patterns is available.
Character: Gentle, affectionate and loyal.
Grooming: 🏠🏠
Breed stereotype: ● 🛋️ 👤👤
Health: No specific reported problems.
Notes: LaPerms are bald or only lightly furred at birth and develop their thick coat later. Rare outside the US.

MANX

Physical description: Medium, cobby with no tail. Soft, smooth fur with dense double coat. All colours and patterns but not points.
Character: Sweet, intelligent and talkative.
Grooming: 🏠🏠
Breed stereotype: ● ● 🐱 💥 🎵
Health: Skeletal defects associated with taillessness.
Notes: Often said to exhibit dog-like behaviour, such as fetching, following and growling at intruders. Longhaired variety is called the Cymric.

MUNCHKIN

Physical description: Medium and cobby with extremely short legs. Coat is silky and can be short or long. A variety of colours and patterns is available.
Character: Sociable and affectionate.
Grooming: 🏠🏠
Breed stereotype: ● ● 🛋️ 👤👤
Health: Skeletal defects.
Notes: A controversial breed that is still very rare. Not recognized by all breeding and showing associations because of the objection to the intentional breeding of genetic deformity.

OCICAT

Physical description: Medium to large and moderate. Fine and flat coat with spotted tabby pattern in a range of colours. Dark-outlined eyes.
Character: Gentle, friendly and energetic.
Grooming: 🏠
Breed Stereotype: ● ● 🐱 👤👤
Health: No specific reported problems.
Notes: The Ocicat is not the product of hybrid breeding with wild cats, as is often thought.

ORIENTAL SHORTHAIR**

Physical description: Medium, extreme foreign with a very short, silky coat in nearly all patterns and colours except pointed. Green eyes.
Character: Lively, playful and inquisitive.
Grooming: 🏠
Breed stereotype: ● ● ● 🐱 🎵
Health: Reported liver and eye disorders.
Notes: In the UK, the white Oriental Shorthair is called the Foreign White and the deep brown is called the Havanna. In the US, the Havanna Brown is considered a different breed.

RUSSIAN BLUE**

Physical description: Medium and moderate. A short, seal-like, dense coat that sticks out from the body. Blue with some white-tipped guard hairs that create a sheen. Green eyes.
Character: Placid, sensitive and quiet.
Grooming: 🏠🏠
Breed stereotype: ● ● 🛋️ 💥
Health: No specific reported problems.
Notes: Thought to have come to Britain from the port of Archangel in Russia as early as the 1600s, it is also known as the Archangel Cat or Foreign Blue. The Nebelung is a longhaired variety of the Russian Blue but is still rare outside Russia.

SCOTTISH FOLD

Physical description: Medium, cobby build with a round head, wide eyes and ears folded forwards. Short-, medium- or longhaired with a dense, plush coat that sticks out. All colours and patterns except pointed.

Character: Respectful, sweet and friendly.

Grooming:

Breed stereotype: ● ● ●

Health: Skeletal defects.

Notes: All kittens are born with straight ears, but by four weeks old some, though not all, of the litter will have developed folded ears. Not recognized by all breeding and showing associations because of the objection to the intentional breeding of genetic deformity.

SELKIRK REX

Physical description: Medium to large and cobby. Dense, soft, loosely curled fur in both short- and longhaired varieties. All colours and patterns are available.

Character: Intelligent, affectionate and tolerant.

Grooming:

Breed stereotype: ●

Health: No specific reported problems.

Notes: Still quite rare, this breed originated in the US in the late 1980s. At about six months of age the Selkirk Rex develops a much straighter coat, but it curls up again when the cat matures.

SIAMESE**

Physical description: Medium and either extreme foreign or traditional foreign. Very shorthaired, silky coat. Pointed in a range of colours and patterns. Blue eyes.

Character: Determined, extrovert and intelligent.

Grooming:

Breed stereotype: ● ● ●

Health: Reported liver, nervous system, respiratory and eye disorders.

Notes: A very old breed, they used to be kept by the Siamese (Thai) royal family and are the subject of many myths. Although the extreme variety is king of the show world, the much softer looking traditional (or Applehead) Siamese is still being bred.

SINGAPURA*

Physical description: Small and moderate with very short, fine fur. Brown, ticked coat with tabby stripes on the insides of the legs and a lighter undercarriage. All eye colours but blue.

Character: Affectionate, sociable and inquisitive.

Grooming:

Breed stereotype: ● ● ●

Health: No specific reported problems.

Notes: Also known as the Drain Cat of Singapore, this is the smallest breed of cat.

SNOWSHOE

Physical description: Medium and moderate with a short, glossy coat. Pointed pattern in typical Siamese colours (lilac, chocolate, seal, blue) with blue eyes and four white paws.

Character: Docile, affectionate and intelligent.

Grooming:

Breed stereotype: ● ●

Health: No specific reported problems.

Notes: An American breed that was created by crossing a Siamese and an American Shorthair; still quite rare.

SPHYNX**

Physical description: Medium and moderate with very large ears. Called hairless but actually has a soft, sparse, downy coat. All colours and patterns (except tipped or ticked patterns).

Character: Lively, affectionate and playful.

Grooming:

Breed stereotype: ● ● ●

Health: No specific reported problems.

Notes: The Sphynx must be kept warm in the winter and out of the sun in the summer and so is usually kept indoors.

TONKINESE*

Physical description: Medium and moderate. Short, fine and silky coat that lies flat. Pointed pattern, with blue or green eyes.

Character: Intelligent, playful and sociable.

Grooming:

Breed stereotype: ● ● ●

Health: Reported kidney, respiratory and gum disorders.

Notes: Siamese x Burmese cross.

How to Find Your Cat

Where to look

Non-pedigree cats can be found through rehoming charities, classified adverts, friends, or one may just find you! Pedigrees are available almost solely through breeders, although rehoming organizations will have pedigree cats from time to time.

NON-PEDIGREES

There are thousands of non-pedigree cats and kittens waiting to be rehomed all over the world, the result of abandonment and a widespread failure to neuter cats. If you are not concerned with pedigree breeding, you'll find all ages, colours, shapes and sizes, and all deserving of loving new homes. To find your nearest **adoption centre** you could search the internet or a phone book. Or you could contact a **cat welfare charity** to ask for advice (contact details appear on page 126).

You may see **classified adverts** in your local paper, but take care buying from these sources. Some breeders can be unscrupulous 'kitten farmers' with no regard for the health of their cats or kittens, so research carefully any breeder that you are thinking of buying from. You could also ask your local **vets** if they know of any non-pedigree kittens available in your area.

PEDIGREES

A pedigree registration council, such as the **GCCF**, should be able to help you find a breeder for most of the different pedigree breeds (contact details appear on page 126). **Cat magazines** often contain classifieds where breeders advertise new kittens and many breeders have **websites**. **Cat shows** are the best place to meet different breeders.

Take the opportunity to ask questions, as most breeders will enjoy talking about their particular breed. Pedigrees up for rehoming are rare, but **breed clubs and charities** sometimes have them.

How to choose

Once you have considered all the different shapes, sizes and characters available to you and which would suit you best, you then have to go and select the cat or kitten. If you are going for a pedigree, most of your decisions will have been made before you pick your kitten. If you are rehoming, there will be some choosing left to do. Quite often, in the end, one cat just feels like the 'right one'.

REHOMING A CAT OR KITTEN

When you rehome from a charity, you will probably have quite a variety of shapes, sizes, colours, sexes and ages to choose from. This is where all the questions you have asked yourself about what kind of cat you are looking for will help you to narrow down the choices.

A reputable rehoming charity will discuss what sort of cat you are after and will always disclose any health or behavioural problems that they know a cat has. Adoption centres are not the most natural of environments for cats, no matter how hard charity workers try, so you should take your time and if you like a cat that seems quite shy, stay with him for a while to see if he becomes more confident. Ask the people who work there what the cat is like with people he knows. Usually, once a cat is in his own home, you will find he relaxes far more.

Rehoming a cat from a charity means you'll have the benefit of knowing he has been vet checked, vaccinated, microchipped and, in most cases, neutered. Many charities like to carry out home visits prior to rehoming, so both you and they can be confident that the cat you have chosen will fit in. You'll also get lots of support and advice, so all you'll need to worry about is settling in your new cat.

Cats Protection

Cats Protection is the UK's largest cat welfare charity. It rehomes over 55,000 cats and kittens nationwide each year and has around 7,000 unwanted and abandoned cats waiting for homes at any one time.

BUYING A KITTEN FROM A BREEDER

First you will have to contact the breeder and tell them what you are looking for. Pedigree kittens are judged by the breeder as either show, breeding or pet quality. Breeders are unlikely to sell breeding-quality kittens to someone they do not know, and even if you want a pet-quality kitten you will probably have to reserve from a future litter and wait. When your litter arrives, arrange to see them, but remember there will be little choice as to colour or sex.

Is the breeder reputable?

When you visit a breeder (whether of pedigrees or moggies) ask as many questions as possible and don't be afraid to have a good look around. Think twice if:

1. There is a strong smell of faeces and urine.

2. The litter trays and bowls are dirty or there is no fresh water.

3. There are too many kittens. A single breeder on their own shouldn't have more than one or two litters at a time. The average litter size is between four and six kittens.

4. The breeder doesn't seem to have a deep knowledge of the breed.

5. The breeder denies or doesn't know that the breed has any hereditary defects or disease associated with it.

6. The breeder will let you take a kitten before it is nine weeks old – kittens should remain with their mother until they are at least eight weeks old.

7. The mother and kittens are kept away from the house and appear very nervous. Kittens should be socialized carefully in a family environment (referred to as being raised 'under foot').

8. The mother or kittens look weak or dull – some mothers do look a bit thin, especially those with large litters.

9. You are not allowed to see the mother.

10. The breeder does not have signed, registered pedigree papers for a cat described as 'pedigree'.

11. The breeder will not be vaccinating the kittens before they leave for new homes.

12. The breeder is trying to pressure you to buy a kitten or doesn't ask you any questions about yourself.

IS THE KITTEN HEALTHY?

Ears should be clean inside with no black grit.

The coat and skin should be soft and healthy, not too oily. There should be no dry patches. Black flecks in the fur suggest fleas.

The head should be steady, not shaking or bobbing.

Eyes should be bright and clear, not red or weeping. The third eyelid should not be permanently visible at the inner corner of the eye.

The bottom should be clean. without faeces or dampness.

Nose should be moist but not runny. Sneezing or wheezing suggests illness.

Gums should be pink and teeth should be clean.

The kitten should appear alert and calm, not terrified or listless.

Movement should be free.

There shouldn't be an excessive pot belly – this may suggest worms.

Chapter 2

ALL ABOUT YOUR CAT

Cats and humans, two of the most successful mammals on the planet, have formed a bond that reaches to every corner of the earth. Evidence shows that cats and humans were living together as long as 9,500 years ago, cats protecting the human harvest and humans providing cats with food and shelter. This fragile alliance has lasted through war, famine and plague. From the sacred cats of ancient Egypt to the witches' familiars of the medieval world, cats have had to survive many of man's superstitions. But the mysteries that surround cats – their nine lives, their sixth sense, the luck and misfortune they bring – are really only our attempts to explain their incredible abilities.

Your cat can hear you coming long before you ever know he's there, can jump several times his own height and land quite comfortably on a single fencepost, and can see in almost total darkness. He can sleep for sixteen hours a day, but is always alert. He can appear without making a sound, then disappear again just as suddenly without you ever seeing him go. It is this incredible mastery of movement and extraordinary sensory ability that make the domestic cat such an intriguing and mysterious creature.

Fortunately for cats, human beings today have a far better understanding of the feline world. Learning as much as you can about your cat – his history, his abilities and the way he communicates – is all part of appreciating him for the remarkable creature he is, and becoming a better cat owner in the process.

WHERE YOUR CAT COMES FROM

All cats, from the lion to the tabby, owe their existence to the same ancestors millions of years ago. Not many fossils remain of either prehistoric cats or ancient domestic cats, but scientists have gathered enough evidence to piece together a timeline of events in the history of the cat.

65 million years ago . . .
Dinosaurs become extinct and mammals become the dominant life form on the planet.

30 million years ago . . .
Proailurus, or 'the first true cat', evolves from a tree-dwelling insect-eater. It is known to have lived in western Europe.

12 million years ago . . .
Cats start to develop into the five different groups that we know today – Neofelis (the clouded leopard), Lynx (including the lynx and bobcat), Panthera (including the tiger, lion, leopard and jaguar), Acinonyx (the cheetah) and Felis (including the European wildcat, the African wildcat, the Pallas cat and our very own domestic cat).

10,000 years ago . . .
Farming settlements begin to spring up in the Fertile Crescent of the Middle East (present-day Iraq, Syria, Israel and Lebanon). Villages store seed and grain, attracting mice which flourish on the large supplies of food and begin to multiply.
  When a few brave wildcats realize there is a good supply of mice in the villages, they risk confrontation with man to hunt them. The cats prove to be useful in keeping the food safe, so the humans encourage them to stay.

9,500 years ago . . .
A man and his cat are buried together in Cyprus. The island didn't have an indigenous cat population so people must have taken them there.

4,000–3,900 years ago
The ancient Egyptians start keeping cats in large numbers to protect their harvests. Cats begin to play a very important role in the religion and culture of the time.

3,500–3,000 years ago
The ancient Egyptians worship cats as gods and try to prevent any other nation from acquiring them. But when traders see how valuable cats are in controlling rodents, they smuggle them up the Nile to the coast. From there, Greek and Phoenician traders take cats with them on their ships to the European mainland and the Middle East.

2,500–1,500 years ago
Cats spread throughout Europe and Asia, through both trade and the expansion of the Roman Empire.

1,500–600 years ago
The Christian church suspects cats are evil and starts a campaign to wipe them out. The drop in cat numbers allows rat populations to soar and rats help spread the plague that kills nearly a quarter of Europe's population in the Middle Ages.

500 years ago to the present day
The cat gains favour once more and eventually completes his domination of the world when he travels by ship to America with the early settlers. By the late 1800s domestic cats are found everywhere there are human beings and, as man discovers other means of keeping food safe from pests, their relationship changes from one of working to one of companionship.

Present day
Cats overtake dogs in the USA in the 1980s and in the UK in the 1990s to become the world's most popular pet.

BRAIN, NERVES AND GLANDS

The brain, nerves and glands help to sense what is going on inside and outside your cat's body, decide if a reaction is needed and then cause the reaction to happen. Everything a cat does, from pouncing on prey to breathing, is controlled by these systems.

Your cat's control centre

Just like yours, your cat's brain is his control centre. It assesses all the information sent to it and sends out 'instructions' to the body. Different parts of the brain are in charge of dealing with different information.

Cerebrum – the cat's intelligence centre, split into four different lobes:

- the **parietal lobe** processes senses like taste, touch and temperature.

- the **occipital lobe** processes visual information.

- the **temporal lobe** processes sound and memory.

- the **frontal lobe** is responsible for making decisions (e.g. on moving, etc.).

Olfactory bulb – processes smells.

Cerebellum – deals with co-ordination of movement and balance.

Spinal cord – carries messages to and from the brain and the nerves.

Hypothalamus – the communication hub of the nerves and glands.

Pituitary gland – the 'master' gland, controlling all the others.

Your cat's brain is tiny in comparison to yours. It is about 5 cm long and weighs approximately 30 g – that is just under 1 per cent of his body weight, whereas your brain is more than 2 per cent of your body weight. Cat and human brains look very similar in shape but are differently proportioned.

Your cat's cerebrum is a smaller part of his brain than yours is, as his thought processes and emotions are much less complex. In particular his frontal and temporal lobes are much less developed than yours: he does not reason or make complex decisions and, although his hearing is very good, he cannot decipher language or remember complicated things.

On the other hand, your cat's cerebellum is only slightly smaller than his cerebrum and so proportionally is much larger than yours, giving him his superior abilities in movement and balance. Similarly, his olfactory bulb is much more developed than yours in comparison to total brain size, enabling him to smell so acutely.

GLANDS AND NERVES

Just like you, communication between your cat's brain and the rest of his body is carried out by glands and nerves. **Glands** release **hormones** (chemical messages) into the blood, causing particular organs to react. There are a number of different glands, each producing different hormones. The system of glands is called the **endocrine system**.

Among other things, glands are responsible for producing insulin to control sugar levels in the blood after your cat has eaten, and adrenalin to increase his heart rate if he needs to run away from danger. If a gland doesn't work properly, it can lead to illness such as diabetes or hyperthyroidism (see pages 87 and 90).

Nerves relay information and work extremely quickly. **Sensory nerves** sense things like pain, temperature or light, and tell the brain what they feel or see. **Motor nerves** take messages from the brain to different parts of the body, such as the muscles, to tell them what to do. The group of nerves that goes up and down the spine is called the **spinal cord**.

What happens when you step on your cat's tail

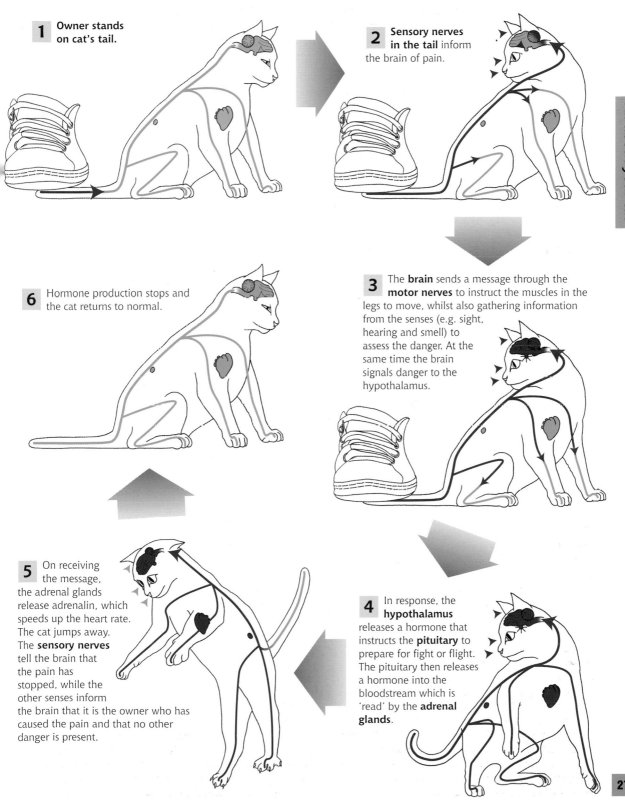

1 Owner stands on cat's tail.

2 **Sensory nerves in the tail** inform the brain of pain.

3 The **brain** sends a message through the **motor nerves** to instruct the muscles in the legs to move, whilst also gathering information from the senses (e.g. sight, hearing and smell) to assess the danger. At the same time the brain signals danger to the hypothalamus.

6 Hormone production stops and the cat returns to normal.

5 On receiving the message, the adrenal glands release adrenalin, which speeds up the heart rate. The cat jumps away. The **sensory nerves** tell the brain that the pain has stopped, while the other senses inform the brain that it is the owner who has caused the pain and that no other danger is present.

4 In response, the **hypothalamus** releases a hormone that instructs the **pituitary** to prepare for fight or flight. The pituitary then releases a hormone into the bloodstream which is 'read' by the **adrenal glands**.

27

SKIN AND FUR

Your cat's skin forms a barrier between his body and the outside world, while his fur gives him camouflage, physical protection and warmth.

Your cat's skin structure

Your cat's skin is almost totally waterproof; it protects the more delicate inner body from infection and the elements. Unlike yours, your cat's skin is only loosely attached to the structure underneath it, thus allowing him to move his head and limbs much more than you can.

The outer part of the skin (the **epidermis**) is made up of many layers of cells. Older cells form the strong, flexible outer layer. The old cells gradually break up and fall off, and younger cells replace them from below.

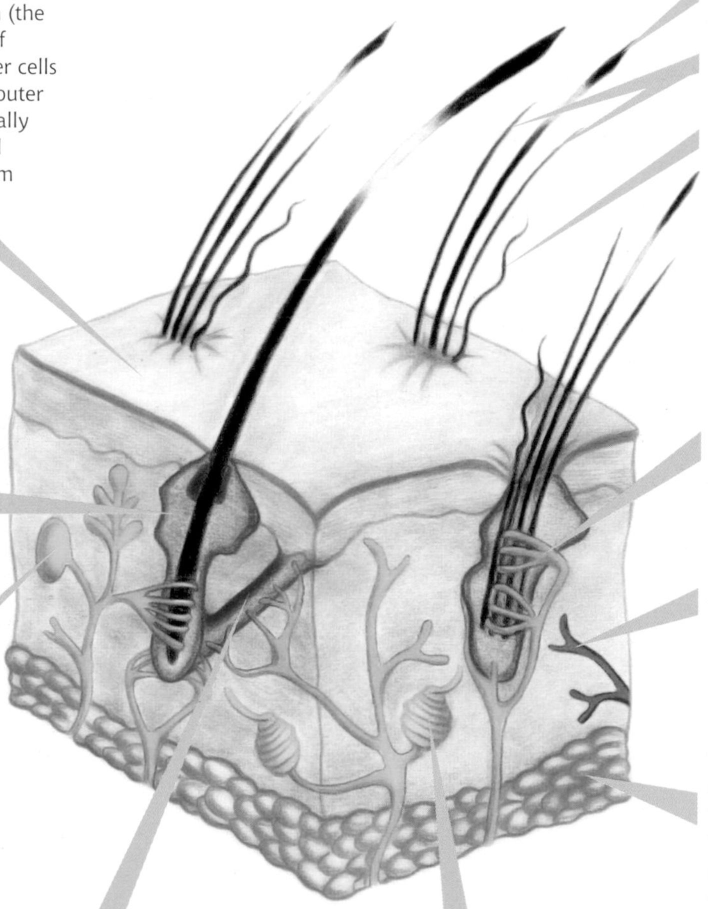

Each hair grows from a pouch (or **follicle**) in the surface of the skin.

Small glands (called **sebaceous glands**) release an oily substance on to the skin and hairs to stop them from getting too dry.

Guard hair – outer layer

Awn hair – middle layer

Down hair – inner layer

Nerves transmit sensations and instructions between the skin and brain.

Blood vessels transport oxygen and carbon dioxide to and from the skin cells.

The **hypodermis** consists of a layer of fat cells that sit below the skin. The tissue provides insulation and an energy store.

Small muscles (**arrector pili muscles**) are attached to each hair follicle. When they are triggered (e.g. by temperature or fear) the muscle pulls on the follicle to make the hair stand up.

Sweat glands help your cat to cool down in hot weather. They occur only in the skin on his paws, so if you see him licking his paws in hot weather, he is just trying to cool off. Other glands on the skin, concentrated under the chin, on the temples and at the base of the tail, are thought to be responsible for releasing **pheromones**, which are chemical messages about the individual cat which other cats can 'read' – see 'Communication', page 41.

Your cat's fur

Fur grows from almost all of your cat's skin to form his coat. As well as being a thick protective layer, the coat also provides insulation from hot, cold and wet conditions. In addition, the coat gives the cat his colour and pattern. For wild or working cats, this is essential camouflage for hunting.

Old fur is continually replaced through moulting or shedding. The amount usually increases when the weather gets hotter in summer, though cats that go outside will probably have a heavier moult in both autumn and spring when they are replacing their fur with a heavier winter or lighter summer coat. Because most homes are now centrally heated, cats kept mainly indoors are likely to shed regularly throughout the year. Longhaired and shorthaired cats moult around the same amount, though very short hair will be less visible around the house.

DIFFERENT TYPES OF HAIRS

Cats can have up to three types of hair on their bodies:

Guard hairs are tough, long and water resistant. They form the outer coat that protects the skin and keeps the more delicate insulating hairs dry.

Awn hairs are rough, helping to insulate and protect.

Down hairs are short, soft and crimped. They trap air to form the insulating undercoat.

Cats also have special extra-thick, long sensory hairs. The most obvious are on the face – the whiskers – but there are also others on other parts of the body, including the backs of the legs. They go much deeper into the skin and are connected to more nerves than normal hairs. See 'Touch', page 40.

guard hair   *awn hair*   *down hair*

When he feels under threat, your cat can make all his hair stand on end so that he looks as big as possible.

Why don't cats like water?

Each hair in your cat's coat is water resistant, but despite this he is not completely waterproof and will eventually become soaked. He will easily lose heat if he is wet, becoming cold and miserable.

In general, though, most cats dislike water simply because they are unused to it. Your cat will prefer to feel in control, so if he is sprayed or dunked in something he is unsure of, he is likely to panic. However, environment and experience play an important part. If a cat is bathed from an early age (see box, page 69), there is no reason why he shouldn't enjoy getting wet.

THE SKELETON

Your cat's skeleton protects his delicate internal organs and nerves, and provides a support structure for the tissue of his body. His skeleton is very light and strong and has some important differences from your own which help him to be flexible and agile.

Your cat's protective structure

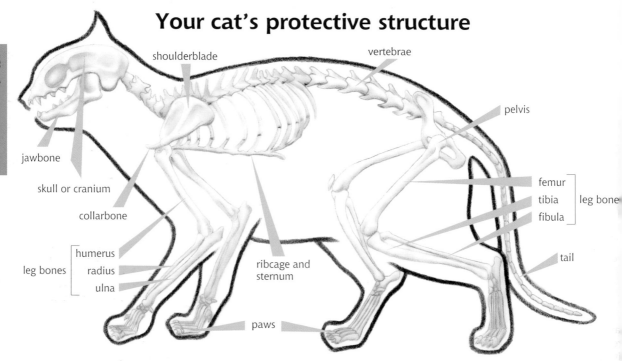

shoulderblade
vertebrae
pelvis
jawbone
skull or cranium
collarbone
femur
tibia
fibula — leg bone
leg bones
humerus
radius
ulna
ribcage and sternum
tail
paws

A cat has around 244 bones (you have about 206). The number varies, depending on whether he has extra toes (see page 32) or is tailless, or on the length of his tail.

The backbone is made up of a series of connected smaller bones (vertebrae) with a hole through their middle. The spinal cord, a group of the most important nerves in the body, passes through this hole so that it is protected.

The skull surrounds the delicate brain and has large holes where the eyes and the inner parts of the ear sit. Your cat's ribcage and sternum form a protective cage around his vital organs, the heart and lungs.

Broken bones

Cats are most likely to break bones when falling from a height (see page 35) or being hit by a car. However, your cat's suppleness and agility mean he can get himself out of most potential bone-breaking situations.

Many surgeons have noted that not only do cats suffer broken bones less often than dogs, but they heal far faster too. In the wild, cats are mostly solitary, whereas dogs live in social groups and so do not depend only on themselves for survival, so it stands to reason that cats would have evolved with faster healing techniques. A cat who healed quickly would have survived, whereas one who couldn't would probably have died, leaving the stronger genes to be passed on to the next generations.

Flexibility and strength

The individual bones in your cat's backbone are joined by cartilage – a smooth, flexible material. These joints are far more supple in him than they are in you, allowing him to curl in a tight ball comfortably. He also has around 53 vertebrae, whereas you have only about 33 of which four are fused, and human vertebrae are more tightly packed than a cat's. This too means that he can bend and twist himself in ways that you never could.

Unlike yours, a cat's shoulderblades are not connected to his backbone via his collarbones, and his collarbones are not connected to any other bones directly – instead they are supported by a network of muscles. This lack of rigid structure gives your cat a very narrow, flexible body. This helps him squeeze through spaces that look too small, flatten himself against the floor and turn his front legs in almost any direction.

Your cat's bones are fine and light, enabling him to jump, climb and change direction at high speed easily. His skeleton is also very strong, so it can withstand the force of landing or braking suddenly without getting damaged.

MUSCLES

Your cat has over 500 muscles. They primarily control his movement, but are also responsible for internal functions such as the contraction of the heart to pump blood around the body. Your cat's muscles are far more supple and flexible than yours and are perfectly evolved for silent, controlled stalking followed by a huge burst of energy.

Your cat's muscles

There are 32 muscles in your cat's ear compared to just six in yours. He can rotate each ear 180° independently of the other, which gives him excellent hearing. See also 'Hearing, Balance and the Ears', page 34.

Hip and hindquarter muscles are large and strong, helping your cat to pounce, run and jump.

'INVISIBLE' MUSCLES

Like us, a cat also has 'involuntary' muscles that keep his internal organs working without him being conscious of it. There are two types of these: cardiac (the heart muscles) and smooth (the intestines, stomach and bladder).

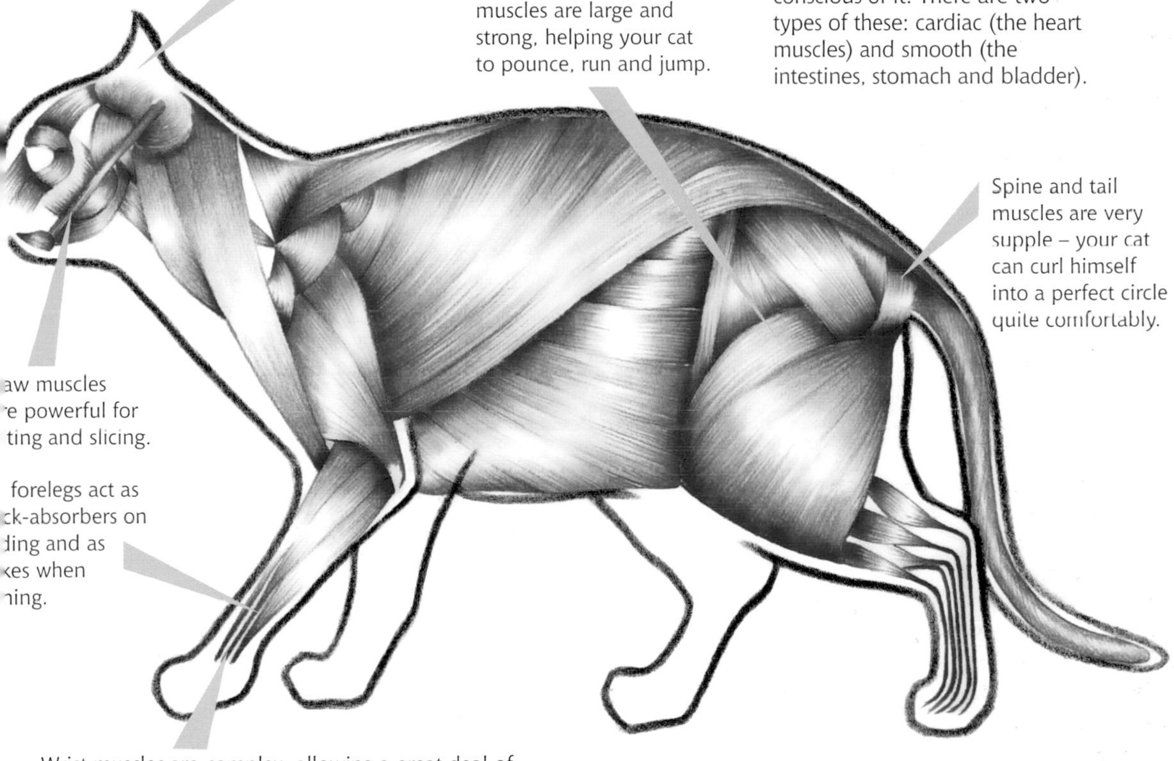

Spine and tail muscles are very supple – your cat can curl himself into a perfect circle quite comfortably.

...aw muscles
...e powerful for
...ting and slicing.

...forelegs act as
...ck-absorbers on
...ding and as
...es when
...ing.

Wrist muscles are complex, allowing a great deal of movement of the paw. This helps the cat to balance on very small and odd-shaped surfaces without much difficulty.

Your cat is an acrobat

Your cat is quite capable of jumping several times his own height to land comfortably perched in a 15 cm^2 space from a standing start. He can leap over six times his length in a single bound and can become completely motionless in an instant. He is also an excellent climber and, for short bursts, can run at 30 m.p.h., changing direction in a moment.

The muscles that help him do all this are called **striated muscles**. Your cat has a huge network of these strong, supple muscles throughout his body. They generally work in pairs on a joint, each one contracting to move the limb one way or another when his brain sends the signal.

Your cat is a sprinter

Cats have three types of muscle cells: slow-acting cells; fast-acting cells that tire out quickly; and some fast-acting cells that tire out slowly. Your cat's muscles are mainly made of the first two. So, although he can run, jump and twist better than any gymnast, he cannot keep doing it for very long because he does not have a lot of stamina and his muscles get tired.

PAWS AND CLAWS

Your cat's paws are nimble, lethal and silent, giving him his excellent balance and agility, and allowing him to creep up on prey unannounced and catch it easily.

Agility and balance

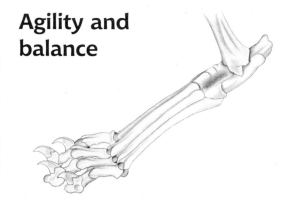

Your cat's paws and claws act as shock-absorbers when he runs or jumps, as crampons when he climbs and as knives when he hunts.

He has five toes on each front paw and four on each back paw. The bones in his paws and legs roughly correspond to those in your arms and legs but, while you walk on the soles of your feet, your cat always walks on his toes. This is because the bones in your feet that lie flat against the ground – from the ball of your foot to your heel – correspond to the bones in the lower part of your cat's leg; the bend you see halfway up his hind leg is the equivalent of your heel. This allows him ultimate control over his movement and the ability to spring into action at a moment's notice.

Your cat walks silently

Your cat is specially equipped so that he can walk silently. To cushion his paws and ensure that he makes as little noise as possible when he walks, he has soft, velvety pads of tough skin on each paw where no hair grows.

Left paw or right?

When it comes to using their paws to catch or manoeuvre something, cats are usually left-pawed or ambidextrous; only 20 per cent are right-pawed.

Polydactyl cats

Polydactyl cats are born with more than the average number of toes. Despite the myth that polydactyl cats were employed on ships because they could climb the ropes better than ordinary cats, they are not actually affected by the extra toes. The current world record for a polydactyl cat is held by Jake from Canada who has 28 toes instead of the usual 18.

This kitten clearly shows extra toes on both his front and back paws.

Your cat's claws

A cat has a claw on each toe. While a dog's claws are naturally extended all the time, your cat's claws are tucked away and are extended only when needed. This means that they are not always being worn against the floor; he can walk silently and keep his claws sharp at the same time.

Claws grow throughout a cat's life. They have a sensitive inner part (the **quick**) containing blood vessels and an outer 'dead' part made of layers of a protein called keratin. The top layers wear down with use and your cat will scratch or pull at his claws whilst grooming to remove the worn layers, revealing new, sharper layers underneath. Most cats will need some help with keeping their claws trimmed; for more information on this, see page 68.

The fifth claw on the front paws is called the dew claw. It can be found higher up the paw and does not come into contact with the ground, but it is useful when climbing or gripping small prey.

Claws extended

Claws retracted

SMELL AND THE NOSE

For a domestic cat, who doesn't rely on hunting for food, the most important of all the senses is smell. If something unusual is presented to your cat, he will approach cautiously and smell it. This is because he relies on this sense to identify objects, individuals, hazards, sexual partners and food. It is also important for communication with other cats.

How a cat smells

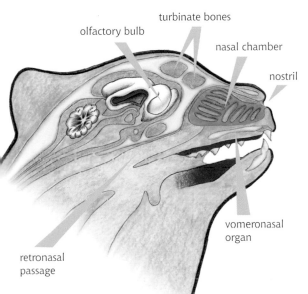

olfactory bulb

turbinate bones

nasal chamber

nostril

vomeronasal organ

retronasal passage

The molecules of an odour are inhaled through the cat's nostrils and are circulated around the nasal chamber and turbinate bones, which are coated with a sticky membrane that collects the odour molecules as they pass by. This membrane is called the **olfactory mucosa** and it contains scent-receptor cells that 'read' the scent and then relay it to the olfactory bulb in the brain (see page 26). The olfactory bulb processes the information and identifies the scent. For a cat, smell is an important part of tasting. When he eats, the smell of the food travels up from the mouth through the retronasal passage to the nasal chamber to be analysed (see page 39).

Your cat has a very sensitive nose

Your cat can smell if you have stroked another cat, even if it was hours ago. He can tell if you haven't washed his food bowl properly and is able to judge if there is even a tiny speck of salt in his water. He has as many as 200 million scent-receptor cells in his nose, whereas you have only around 5 million. With such a good sense of smell, he can easily detect the faintest odour and recognize the individual chemicals in a mixture – so don't be surprised if he seems to have smelled something that you haven't noticed at all.

Your cat has an extra smelling organ

In addition to his nose, your cat has an extra organ for collecting detailed information about a scent. This is called the **vomeronasal organ**, or Jacobson's organ, and it is located at the front of the roof of his mouth. It is connected to the brain via an alternative route to the normal sense of smell. When your cat uses this extra organ, he will wrinkle his nose, open his mouth and raise his upper lip – this is called the Flehmen response. It can look as though he has smelled something bad, but usually it is in response to the smell of another cat, particularly a female in heat.

Dogs, who also rely heavily on their sense of smell, have a vomeronasal organ too. Humans have the remnants of one, but it no longer functions.

Does your cat have a sixth sense?

It has long been thought that cats have amazing sensory abilities, such as being able to tell that there is going to be an earthquake long before the event. Other extraordinary stories include a cat who can foretell the death of residents at a nursing home and one who can sense the onset of his owner's epileptic fits. These strange skills have been attributed to a sixth sense, but are far more likely to be due to your cat's sense of smell and the vomeronasal organ.

HEARING, BALANCE AND THE EARS

Your cat has extraordinary hearing, which is particularly adapted to picking up the high-pitched sounds of small prey. He can tell the difference between almost identical sounds and is able to pinpoint the origin of a sound with accuracy and incredible speed.

How your cat hears

Pinna – the outer part of the ear is like a net that catches sound waves and directs them down the ear canal and towards the eardrum.

Ossicles – these three tiny bones (also known as the hammer, anvil and stirrup) vibrate, then refine and amplify the vibrations, exerting a force on the liquid-filled **cochlea**.

Eardrum – sound waves bounce against the eardrum which vibrates and moves three tiny bones (**ossicles**) positioned behind it.

Vestibular apparatus – the organ of balance.

Auditory nerve – transfers the electrical impulses to the brain.

Cochlea – a shell-like, liquid-filled bone. Vibrations in the liquid affect special cells which translate them into electrical impulses for the auditory nerve to 'hear'.

SOUNDS THAT YOU CAN'T HEAR

Your cat can hear sound frequencies up to 65 kHz, which is the kind of high-pitched noise that a small rodent makes. You can only register sounds up to 20 kHz, but you do not depend on your hearing for food in the same way that your cat does.

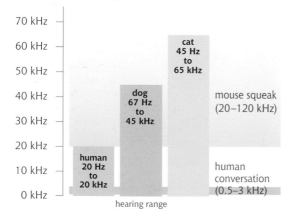

hearing range

- human 20 Hz to 20 kHz
- dog 67 Hz to 45 kHz
- cat 45 Hz to 65 kHz
- mouse squeak (20–120 kHz)
- human conversation (0.5–3 kHz)

ALMOST IDENTICAL SOUNDS

Your cat can differentiate between very similar sounds to a difference of about one-tenth of a tone. He will know the difference between your car and all the other cars that go past during the day; he can tell if the cupboard you've opened is his food cupboard or a different one; and he knows by the sound of your footfall whether it is you or another member of your family who has just walked in.

WHERE A SOUND IS COMING FROM

Because he has 32 ear muscles compared to your six, your cat can move the outer parts of his ears 180 degrees in opposite directions. Being able to move his ears independently like this means that he can hear sounds all around his body without moving his head. It also means that he can pinpoint the exact location of one noise, such as a mouse squeaking, even if there is grass rustling in the wind all around him. In fact, from a metre away, your cat can tell the difference between two different sounds that are only a few centimetres apart and pinpoint the exact location of each.

movement of ears

movement of ears

PRIMARY FIELD OF HEARING

Balance

As well as hearing, part of the inner ear is also responsible for your cat's incredible sense of balance. It helps him to walk along narrow fences, climb trees and land easily.

TIGHTROPE-WALKING

Part of the inner ear, the **vestibular apparatus**, is actually formed of a number of curved canals, sometimes called the semicircular canals. Tiny hairs coat the inner surface of these canals, which are filled with liquid and tiny floating crystals. When your cat moves, the liquid and crystals shift around and move the hairs. The hairs translate the movement into impulses that inform his brain of his exact position in relation to everything around him.

Your cat's inner-ear structure is similar to your own, but his sense of balance is far more exact. Cats developed their balancing skill because, as solitary animals in the wild – unlike dogs, which live in packs – it was important that they learned to climb, not only to catch tree-dwelling prey but also so that they could hide their catch from ground-living animals and sleep safely away from predators. Combined with his superior muscular and skeletal systems, your cat's sense of balance makes him a formidable hunter and all-round acrobatic master.

FALLING ON HIS FEET

It is widely believed that cats always land on their feet. This is not always the case: falling can kill your cat very easily, so you should never allow him access to balconies or high open windows. However, there is a reason for the belief, and it lies in what is known as your cat's 'righting reflex'.

Quite often, cats survive high and low falls but don't survive medium falls (around 6–20 metres). This is because medium falls exert a lot of force on the cat's body as he lands, but don't give him enough time for the righting reflex to work, so he may land awkwardly. Also, just because a cat lands on his feet, it doesn't mean that he is not hurt: injuries from falls can range from broken bones to massive internal damage.

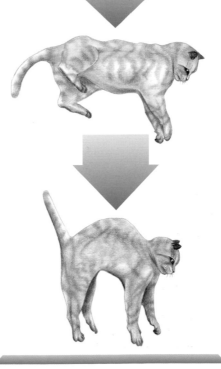

On falling, your cat's sense of balance and his vision report to his brain that he is not the right way up.

His brain instructs the head to turn so the balance organs are the right way up. Once the head has turned, the brain is informed that the head is in the correct position by the balance organs and by the eyes, which can spot the approaching ground.

Once the head is in the correct position, the brain instructs the shoulders and forelimbs to stretch forwards and out. This helps your cat maintain the correct position in relation to the ground and helps to slow his fall.

Next, your cat's tail swings out and around, followed by his back legs, so that the whole body is the correct way up.

Now the right way up, your cat's legs are pushed outwards to slow his fall even more. Then he bends his legs a bit and relaxes his muscles to prepare for impact on the ground.

Record falls

The highest recorded fall survived by a cat was reported in the *New York Times* in 1994, when a cat in Manhattan fell 46 floors – more than 140 metres – and lived. Prior to that, the record was held by a Miami cat called Andy, who survived a fall of 61.5 metres.

SIGHT

Your cat's eyes work in the same way as your own but with a few key differences that help him spot prey in the dark.

Your cat has a wide field of vision and can see light and movement with ease. But he can't see colour as well as you and finds it difficult to focus on details. Cats have evolved like this because, as nocturnal hunters, it is important that they spot movement in bad light but not so important that they can see the colour or detail of their prey.

How a cat sees

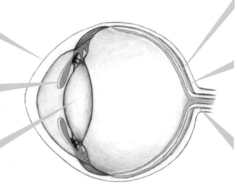

Cornea – light passes through this protective layer, which directs the light towards the pupil and iris.

Iris – the iris (the coloured part) expands or contracts to let the right amount of light through the hole in its centre (the pupil) and into the lens.

Lens – the clear, lentil-shaped lens is behind the pupil. It changes shape to direct and focus the light on to the retina.

Retina – this layer of cells at the back of the eye collects and 'reads' light. If light gets past these cells, it hits the *tapetum lucidum*.

Tapetum lucidum – this mirror reflects any missed light back on to the retina for a second time. The retina then sends all the information to the optic nerve.

Optic nerve – the optic nerve transports all the gathered information about the position, brightness and colour of everything the cat sees to the brain, which creates a picture.

Your cat can see better in the dark than you

Cats evolved to hunt at night, dawn or dusk, so they see better than humans can in low light. They are able to do this because of the shape of their pupils, the number of light-gathering cells in their retina and a reflective layer of cells in their eyes. However, even though your cat needs only a tiny bit of light to see, just like you he cannot see in total darkness.

In darkness your cat (left) sees much more than you (right).

PUPILS

The pupil is the hole in the eye that allows light to pass through to get to the retina. Like yours, your cat's pupils can change size to control how much light gets through. Unlike yours, his pupils can also change shape – from just a small slit in very bright sunlight to a very large circle in the dark. This means that your cat can see quite clearly in both glaring sun and almost total darkness. Cats' pupils adjust size and shape very fast, so if your cat moves from a dark shed to a bright sunlit garden, his eyesight will adjust to the change of light in seconds.

Because we have evolved to function in the day and sleep at night, humans' eyes don't change size nearly as much as cats' eyes do, and don't change shape at all.

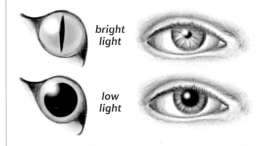

bright light

low light

THE LIGHT-SENSING CELLS

There are two types of cells in the retina. One type – called the **rods** – picks up light; the other – called the **cones** – picks up colour. Your cat has far more rods than cones so is able to pick up tiny amounts of light that you would find impossible to detect.

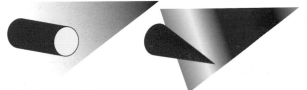

rod cells sense light

cone cells sense colour

THE REFLECTIVE LAYER

Behind the light-gathering rods in your cat's eyes is a layer of reflective cells. This is like a mirror, reflecting light back on to the rods and so giving your cat two chances to see. You don't have this reflective layer of cells in your eyes, but other night predators, such as wolves and foxes, do.

If you take a photo of your cat with a flash, you should see his eyes glowing in the dark. What you are seeing is light reflecting off the mirror in his eyes. This amazing ability inspired Yorkshireman Percy Shaw to invent the famous 'cat's eyes' that reflect car lights back at the driver, improving road safety.

Your cat can't see colour as well as you

Your cat can see blue and green better than red and orange, but all colours look much duller to him than they do to you. This is because he has far more rods than colour-sensing cones in his retina.

Through your cat's eyes (left), colours are much less intense than they are through yours (right).

Your cat has a better field of vision than you

Without moving his head, your cat can see 285 degrees round his body. You can see about 210 degrees, while a rabbit has almost 360-degree vision.

The difference between you, your cat and the rabbit is that you and your cat are essentially predators whereas a rabbit is prey. Predators' eyes sit on the front of the face, looking forwards so that both eyes can see the same scene. Cats' eyes are high up and point slightly outwards, which means they can see more than humans. Seeing with both eyes makes it easier to judge distances and so makes pouncing more accurate. A prey animal has its eyes on either side of its head to give it a wide field of vision for spotting predators, but it can see almost nothing with both eyes and so cannot judge distances very well.

Both you and your cat have blind spots behind your heads and low down in front of your noses. Your cat makes up for these blind spots by being able to move his head almost all the way round, like an owl. You do not have this ability, although you can move your eyeballs much more than your cat can.

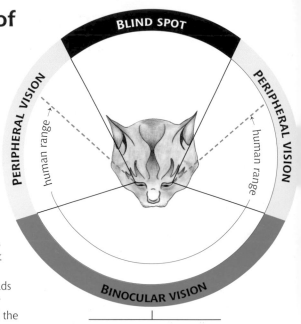

2–6-metre optimum range

Your cat can see movement but not detail

Your cat can spot movement anywhere in his range of vision, but he can't see details well. You can refocus your eyes on various objects at different distances. Your cat, however, can only refocus slightly and he sees things best that are between 2 and 6 metres in front of him – the distance to which he can comfortably run, pounce or jump to catch prey; any further and it is not worth the effort.

Cats can spot movement so easily because their light-sensing cells, which see even tiny changes in light and contrast, can pick out shades of light – that is, prey – moving against a static background.

Your cat (left) can track movement much better than you (right).

Your cat has three eyelids

Cats have a third eyelid, positioned behind the outer pair. It closes from side to side, lubricating and clearing dust from the eye and providing extra protection. It is usually only visible for a moment as your cat opens and closes his eyes. If it becomes permanently visible (as shown above), it can be a sign of illness.

TASTE AND THE MOUTH

Your cat is perfectly adapted to eat just one thing – meat. He has a limited sense
of taste and specialized teeth because of his specific diet. He depends more on his
sense of smell than on his sense of taste to determine whether food is good or not.

Your cat's sense of taste

Whereas humans have evolved to eat a large range of
foods, cats have evolved to eat fresh meat only and so
your cat doesn't have or need as many taste buds as you.

This also means that your cat is unlikely to be fond of
sweet foods, because most cats are not very sensitive to
sweet sensations. He will prefer foods that contain the
sour, bitter and salt tastes that occur in meat.

Having a limited sense of taste doesn't disadvantage
your cat, however, because he is perfectly evolved to find
the food he needs. What he lacks in taste he makes up for
in smell (page 33), and it is this sense that he will use first
to test the palatability of food. He will put something in
his mouth only when he is happy that he cannot smell
anything that might be hazardous to his health.

Once food touches his tongue, the taste buds begin to
process the flavours, but at the same time the smell of
the food is being transferred up to the scent-receptor
cells in the nasal chamber through a passage in the
mouth called the **retronasal passage** (see page 33).
Smelling food in this way when you eat is important for
both you and your cat, which is why both of you can go
off your food if you have a blocked nose.

Teeth made for meat

Your cat's teeth reflect the fact that he is a hunter by
nature. He has two large canine teeth at the front for
killing prey and two teeth (the **carnassial pair**) at the back
of the jaw that work like scissors to cut up meat. Although
he has molars, originally designed for grinding food, he
cannot move his jaw from side to side – a movement
needed to eat large amounts of vegetable matter.

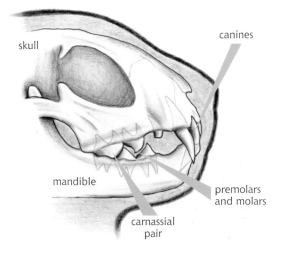

skull

canines

mandible

premolars
and molars

carnassial
pair

Your cat has a multi-purpose tongue

Your cat's tongue is covered with around 250 tiny,
tough, backward-facing hooks called **papillae**, giving it
the texture of sandpaper. As well as containing the taste
buds, the tongue has many other important functions:

Grooming. When your cat grooms himself, the papillae
hooks are stroked across the fur to dislodge loose hairs
and smooth or clean the coat.

Eating. The papillae are so strong that when a cat licks
the carcass of his prey, the tongue can be used to pull
meat from the bones.

Drinking. Your cat will lap water using his tongue, which
he forms into a spoon shape and flicks backwards,
scooping water into his mouth.

TOUCH

Your cat has the same kind of nerves as you, and can feel pressure, pain and temperature.
He hides his pain well and is able to withstand a greater range of temperature than you.
He is also equipped with extra-sensitive hairs to help him feel his way around.

Your cat's body is covered in sensitive nerves

Your cat's entire body is served by nerves that constantly report to his brain about the environment around him. These nerves are most concentrated in the nose and paws, because these are the parts of the cat that always go first into a situation. The nerves sense pain, pressure and temperature and, just as you would drop a pan if you picked it up and found it was hot, they will cause your cat to react suddenly if they experience too much of any of these sensations. This is an automatic lifesaving technique.

It can be difficult to tell if your cat is in pain

Your cat releases large amounts of natural painkillers called **endorphins** into his bloodstream when he feels pain. His endorphin-producing system is far more efficient than in many other animals (including humans) in masking his pain and allowing him to function relatively normally. In the wild, this means that an injured cat avoids attracting the attention of rivals or predators, but in a home it makes it difficult to see whether a cat is suffering. In contrast, dogs, which are social animals, will whine to attract the attention of their companions to their situation.

The most common way for a cat to react to pain is to direct aggression towards whoever he thinks is causing it, so you should always visit the vet for a health check if your cat suddenly starts acting aggressively. See page 104.

Your cat is less sensitive to temperature than you

Your cat's ancestors originated in the desert, where excessive daytime heat is followed by a dramatic drop in temperature. Domestic cats have kept some of this insensitivity to heat and cold, and so will often lie very close to a fire or sit in the snow without showing discomfort. Your cat will start to become uncomfortable at temperatures of around 52°C, nearly 10°C higher than the temperature at which you feel too hot. His insulating fur helps him to withstand cooler temperatures, and some domestic cats that evolved in extremely cold climates developed even thicker, longer fur to help them survive.

Your cat's nose is able to sense very slight fluctuations in temperature. He always goes nose first, so this sensitivity can stop him getting into trouble.

Your cat has special sensory hairs

Your cat has very sensitive hairs known as whiskers. They can be found most obviously on his face (above the lips, on the cheeks and above the eyebrows) but there are also some on the back of his legs.

Each whisker is a long, extra-thick hair that goes three times deeper into the skin than an ordinary hair and is surrounded by a network of nerves. Whiskers are extremely sensitive to the slightest change in air pressure and to movement, so they play a vital role in your cat's senses, helping him to 'see' obstacles in the dark, gauge distances between objects and judge when prey is dead. A cat that has lost his whiskers can be disorientated for some time while he re-adjusts to his reduced sensory perception. For this reason, you should never cut your cat's whiskers.

Your cat's whiskers are vital to his sensory perception.

COMMUNICATION

At first, the way your cat communicates, through scent, sound and body language, will seem very subtle and you may not understand him. As you get to know your cat, however, you will begin to recognize more easily the signs he uses to communicate with you.

Your cat can smell messages

Scent is incredibly important to your cat as a means of communication. By rubbing, spraying and clawing his own personal scent on to the things around him, he is leaving a message to any animal that happens to be passing: 'This is mine.' Unfortunately, compared to your cat's sensitive nose you have a terrible sense of smell and so this is one language that you will find difficult to understand. You will, however, be 'talking' to your cat all the time through the scents on your body; he'll certainly know if you've stroked another cat, even if it was hours ago.

RUBBING

At particular points on your cat's body – under the chin, on the forehead and where the tail meets the back – your cat has glands that produce a substance carrying his individual scent. He rubs these parts of his body on things in his environment   including you – to 'mark' them as his own. This is why, if you've

Rubbing up against this stool identifies it as the cat's own.

stroked another cat or showered, your cat will be especially interested in having you stroke him under the chin, because his smell has faded on you and he wants to top it up.

SPRAYING

By spraying short bursts of urine on objects, cats can leave longer-lasting messages marking their territory. Luckily, this form of communication is normally only used outside, where a cat feels most under threat from strangers and where the elements wash scent away more easily. Your cat should feel secure enough inside his home not

This cat is about to spray part of his territory so that other cats know that it is his.

to need to carry out this behaviour. If it does happen inside, it is usually a sign of an unhappy cat. For more on this, see page 102.

SCRATCHING

As well as keeping his muscles and claws in good shape, scratching is also a way for your cat to mark his territory. He has scent glands in his paws, so scratching releases this scent on to the scratched object.

By scratching a cat leaves his scent on objects around him.

Your cat can 'talk'

Your cat can make a range of different noises to get attention. You will soon learn to understand what he means when he makes these different sounds.

Miaow: Adult cats rarely miaow at each other, because they can say everything they need with body language and scent. Kittens do miaow to get their mother's attention and later in life this 'kitten language' comes in handy for talking to humans, who aren't clever enough to understand cat language fully. Cats learn that humans respond well to this noise, so they develop a range of miaows to mean different things, from 'Where are you?' and 'Wake up!' to 'Can I have some?'

Purr: A low, rumbling noise caused by your cat vibrating the muscles of his voicebox as he breathes in and out. It is heard mainly when a cat is contented, but sometimes when he is ill or in pain too.

Chirrup: Like the miaow, this is used in conversation and is half miaow, half purr.

Hiss: A cat will hiss and spit as a warning. If a cat hisses at you, it's best to give him some space because he is getting short on patience.

Caterwaul: This starts as a low growl but then gets higher and lower. It is mostly used when a cat is angry or frightened, but female cats also make this noise when they are ready to mate.

Natural therapy

Certain frequencies of vibration are known to be therapeutic for humans, encouraging bone-growth, healing and relief from pain or inflammation. Cats purr at these frequencies and some scientists have suggested that one of the reasons a cat purrs is to benefit from this natural therapy.

Body language speaks volumes

You'll find your cat's body language strange at first, but it won't take long to recognize what he is trying to tell you.

Relaxed

Eyes: Half closed and blinking.
Ears: Upright and facing slightly out.
Tail: Lying low or flat on the ground.
Body: Relaxed and calm.
Tip: An arched back is usually a sign of defensive behaviour, but if you are stroking your cat's back or he has just woken, he may arch his back simply to stretch.

Defensive

Eyes: Wide open with very wide pupils; he will try to avoid sustained direct eye contact.
Ears: Flattened and pointing down towards the ground.
Tail: Held low or tucked in.
Body: An initial fright will result in the 'witch's cat' display of arched back, bristled fur and hiss – this apparently aggressive act is actually just a display to try to dissuade the aggressor from attacking. A cornered cat who feels under continued threat will tuck into a crouch or roll on to his back to expose his claws.
Tip: Don't confuse a cat that is lying on his back because he is completely comfortable and safe with one that is preparing to defend himself.

Interested

Eyes: Open with pupils wide.
Ears: Upright and facing towards the object of interest.
Tail: Held high and curled forwards, sometimes waving slowly.
Body: Relaxed, upright and facing the object of interest.
Tip: A slowly waving tail is often just a sign of uncertainty or impatience, but a faster swish of the tail means your cat is becoming increasingly annoyed.

Aggressive

Eyes: Pupils narrowed and staring.
Ears: Pointing towards the victim at first, but will be turned backwards and pressed flat against the head just before an attack.
Tail: Low, bristled and flicking from side to side.
Body: An aggressive cat will move towards his victim purposefully and sometimes with a sideways gait to look more imposing and scare the opponent into submission. If this doesn't work he will prepare to attack by lowering his front as he would when stalking prey.
Tip: Staring is aggressive and will often make one cat back down before any physical fighting begins.

Hunting

Eyes: Open, staring and with wide pupils.
Ears: Aimed directly at the source of prey.
Tail: Held straight out and low, often twitching at the tip.
Body: Kept very low to the ground, with slow, deliberate movements.
Tip: You will see your cat's hunting body language if you play with him using a fishing-rod toy that he can stalk.

LIFECYCLE

The average lifespan of a domestic cat is around 16 years. This can be affected by a number of factors, such as diet, exercise, living conditions, whether he is neutered and luck. Cats that live outside in feral colonies have a shorter average lifespan because they are more likely to succumb to starvation, the elements, illness or rivals. A home-kept domestic cat can often live into his twenties and sometimes longer.

Cat years and their human equivalent

KITTEN

Kittens mature very quickly, going from helpless baby to teenage delinquent in just six months. At this stage, cats are energetic and still depend heavily on others. They become sexually active from around four to six months old so need to be neutered sooner rather than later.

Kitten	Human
2 months	1
4 months	9
6 months	12

ADULT

From the age of one, most cats are full grown and start to develop a calmer personality. An adult cat will still be very active, but is wiser and more independent.

Cat	Human
1	16
2	20
3	25
4	30
5	35
6	40
7	45

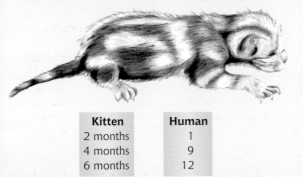

SENIOR

A cat is called a senior from the age of eight, but he is actually middle-aged until he is 13 or 14. As he gets older, he will become a little slower and may put on weight. After 14 years he may begin to suffer from some of the problems of old age – such as sight loss, hearing loss, diabetes or arthritis – but many cats go on to live active and healthy lives well into their later years. See page 94 for more on ageing.

Cat	Human
8	50
9	53
10	56
11	59
12	62
13	65
14	68
15	71
16	74
25	101
35	119

The oldest cat

The cat that holds the Guinness World Record for old age is Creme Puff. Owned by Jake Perry of Austin, Texas, she was born on 3 August 1967 and died on 6 August 2005, just three days after her 38th birthday.

Chapter 3

KEEPING YOUR CAT HAPPY

A happy cat is the most delightful pet – not difficult to care for, cheap to look after and a fun, comforting companion; it's no wonder that the cat has become one of the world's most popular pets. But his independence of spirit and reputation for low maintenance can be built only if you put the right foundations in place. Remember – low maintenance does not mean no maintenance. Far from it.

A cat that lacks basic provisions will not make a good pet – he will become difficult to care for, expensive to look after and, most likely, a poor companion. The basics may seem obvious to you, but it is surprising how often they are overlooked or misunderstood. Cats quickly go downhill without the right food, can become very ill if they don't get the right veterinary treatment and will soon develop bad habits if left without any stimulation. Your new cat may find it hard to admit, but he needs a lot from you: a safe home with access to warmth and shelter, the right food, fresh water, a clean toilet and, preferably, access to the outdoors. Just like you, he may get ill from time to time, so he would benefit from insurance and will need to be registered with a vet.

And, once these things are in place, you will need to spend time with your cat, grooming him, playing games or sitting quietly together. At times like these, you will really see your cat's true character emerging – purring with satisfaction when you come home from work, playing like a kitten when he spots a toy to chase, or snoring contentedly as he sleeps on a pile of clean washing. These shared times are the moments that cat owners treasure – and the good news is, with a happy cat, they are not hard to come by.

THE FIRST FEW WEEKS

You've picked out a perfect cat and it's time to bring him home and introduce him to his new surroundings and family. If he is confident, it may take only a week for your cat to feel happy with his new environment, but a nervous cat may need months to settle properly. If you take time and have patience, however, getting it right in the first few crucial weeks will lay the foundations of trust and you should have a confident, happy cat for life.

Getting ready

Before you rush off to collect your new cat, make sure you have prepared properly for his arrival. First decide on a room where your cat can be left undisturbed by the rest of the family.

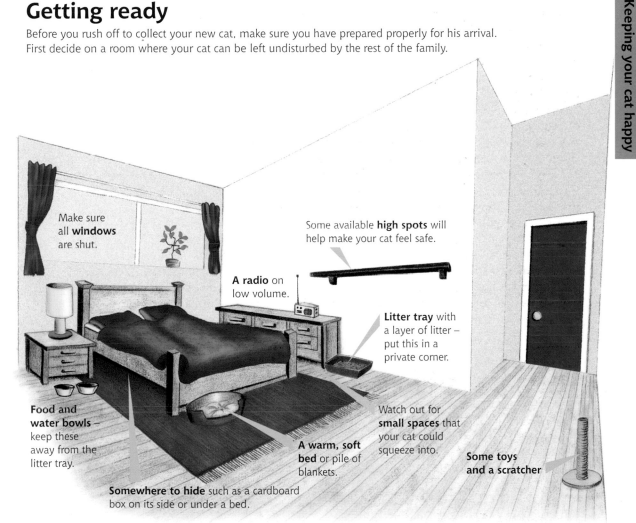

Make sure all **windows** are shut.

Some available **high spots** will help make your cat feel safe.

A radio on low volume.

Litter tray with a layer of litter – put this in a private corner.

Food and water bowls – keep these away from the litter tray.

Watch out for **small spaces** that your cat could squeeze into.

A warm, soft bed or pile of blankets.

Some toys and a scratcher

Somewhere to hide such as a cardboard box on its side or under a bed.

Make sure all the windows and doors in the house are shut and that you have a supply of cat food and litter. Feed him the brand of cat food that he is used to: changing it at this stressful time could cause diarrhoea.

Once you have set up the room and have food and litter, you can go and collect your cat. You must take a secure cat carrier with you (see page 73).

When you arrive to pick up your cat, you will sign and pay for him. Whether you are rehoming a cat or buying a kitten from a breeder, you should receive a starter pack including some basic advice on cat care

and feeding, a vaccination card, a receipt and, usually, six weeks' free insurance to get you started. With a pedigree kitten, you should also be given a registration certificate that proves his pedigree and you may be asked to sign a neutering agreement in which you promise to neuter the kitten when he is old enough.

Some cats will take only days to settle in to their new home, but sometimes it can take weeks or even months. By following the steps on pages 46–48, you can make the process as smooth as possible. Read through all the advice before you start.

Introducing yourself

Step 1

When you get home, let your cat out into his room. Remember that cats rely heavily on scent, so leave his own belongings with him to help him feel at home.

For a cat: Shut the door and let him explore on his own for an hour.

For a kitten: Don't leave him alone until he has settled in. Show him his bowls and litter tray and then go straight to Step 2.

Step 2

The main carer should go in alone at first. Take a newspaper with you. Get down to your cat's level, put out your hand and call his name.

Result 1: He comes to you without hesitation. This means that he is confident around you, so remain with him for a while and then move on to 'Introducing everyone else'.

Result 2: He hesitates to come to you, appears nervous or hides away. Move to Step 3.

Step 3

Never try to force your cat to come out of hiding and don't stare at him. These actions seem threatening to him and will result in a nervous cat defending himself or remaining hidden. Instead, sit on the floor and read your newspaper aloud in low, gentle tones. If there is no improvement after half an hour, try holding out a piece of food or playing with the kind of toy that is attached to string (so you don't get too close).

Result 1: He comes to you. Depending on how confident he seems, you may want to come back later to repeat Step 3. If you are happy that he trusts you, move to 'Introducing everyone else'.

Result 2: He continues to hide. Go away and come back later to repeat Step 3. You may have to repeat this step a number of times before you see any improvement. As long as your cat is eating, drinking and going to the toilet, there's no need to worry.

Don't be surprised if your cat hides from you at first.

Stroking and holding your new cat

Always stroke your new cat gently and watch for the negative signs discussed in 'Communication' (page 41). If you see your cat starting to display signs of impatience, stop and just sit quietly with him.

Always hold a cat under the chest with one hand and support his back legs with the other. It is best not to hold a cat or kitten by the scruff of the neck unless you are used to handling them in this way.

Introducing everyone else

Once your cat is confident with you, you can introduce the rest of the family. Other adults can follow the same steps as above, but children should be supervised. It is easy for children to get excited about a new arrival in the house, but try to keep them calm. Let your cat come to them and, when he does, show the children how to stroke and hold him.

Playing with your cat is a great way to introduce yourself without putting him under too much pressure.

For a cat: Watch for signs of distress. Children without experience may ignore the signs and find themselves on the receiving end of a sharp claw.

For a kitten: Just like babies, kittens should be handled gently and given lots of time off to sleep.

Once your cat is comfortable with everyone, don't allow him to roam around the house before reading 'Introducing other pets' (page 47) if you have other animals. If you do not have any other pets, you can move straight on to 'Exploring the new home' (page 48).

Introducing other pets

In general cats do not find multi-pet living conditions very natural, and most will be quite content to live just with you. Even if you hope that your pets will be best friends, in some cases this simply never happens. However, if your pets don't feel under threat they should be able to live together and may become closer over time. If you have both another cat and a dog, introduce the other cat first.

INTRODUCING CATS TO CATS

Scent is the most important part of feline communication. Each cat has his own scent, so you need to mix these up to create a 'joint scent' throughout the house before they meet face to face. This way they get to know each other without confrontation.

Step 1: Swapping scents

Keep the cats separated so they cannot see each other. You can swap scents in three ways:
* Stroke each cat in turn: don't wash your hands between.
* Swap their bedding.
* Rub your new cat under the chin with a soft cloth, then rub the cloth on corners of walls and furniture at cat height. Do the same with your current cat, but rub the cloth round the new cat's room. When each cat smells the scent of the other he will become very interested in that spot, sniff a lot and may even appear agitated.

Result 1: Your cats stop reacting to each other's scent. Move to Step 2.
Result 2: One of your cats still reacts to the other's scent. Go back and repeat Step 1.

Step 2: Face to face

The next step is to keep your cats separated but let them see each other. The best solution is an interior see-through glass door; next best is a baby or pet gate. If you have neither, wedge the door of your new cat's room open wide enough to see through but not wide enough to get through. If you are using this or a pet gate, remember that cats are very good at jumping and at squeezing through small spaces, so keep a close eye on them.

For a kitten: Follow the steps above but, instead of a barrier, use a see-through cat carrier or kitten cage as your kitten will be able to get through almost any space. Provide him with somewhere in his cage where he can hide from your adult cat. Always supervise kitten–cat meetings until you are certain they are happy with each other.

Result 1: They take a good look at each other but don't react. This is very unlikely at the first face-to-face meeting but can happen. Move to Step 3.
Result 2: They hiss a bit but then quieten down. Let them sit for a while, then close the door and repeat Step 2 later.
Result 3: Both cats panic and run off in opposite directions, or show signs of aggression. Close the door and repeat Step 2 later.

First impressions

It can be difficult – especially when an older cat is bullying a kitten – but you must never punish a cat for his reaction to a newcomer. Ideally, you want each cat to see the other in a positive not a negative light. Feeding them together, giving treats and playing with toys will all help to make their meeting positive.

Step 3: Bringing them closer

Once they seem comfortable with the sight of each other you can start to bring your cats closer. The best way is to feed them at the same time and gradually bring the bowls closer together. Do not take the barrier down yet.

Result 1: They will eat close together without any reaction. Move to Step 4.
Result 2: They hiss a bit but settle down and eat. Repeat Step 3 again until you get no reaction.
Result 3: One or both cats refuses to eat and runs off. Repeat Steps 2 and 3 until you get no reaction.

Step 4: Open introduction

This should be much less of a shock for both of your cats if you have carried out Steps 1–3. First remove the barrier you have been using, then just wait to see what happens. Do not try to push the cats together and don't be concerned if they just avoid each other at first. Try to give both cats plenty of space to run away and hide – do not make them feel closed in, as this may panic them.

Result 1: They hiss a bit but remain calm. This is a great result. Watch them but let them go about their business.
Result 2: They both run off and hide. As long as they settle eventually, you can just keep an eye on them and let them get used to each other over time.
Result 3: They fight. Your cats are unlikely to fight physically, but if they do, don't chase them. Instead, have a blanket to hand that you can put over them to separate them without getting hurt yourself. If you get this result, you should go back to Step 2 and try again.

Full-blown fights are rare between cats, but don't be surprised if there is some hissing and spitting at first.

INTRODUCING CATS TO DOGS

Despite the common stereotype of cats and dogs fighting, it is often easier to introduce a cat to a dog than to another cat. This is because cats naturally lead and dogs naturally follow. So a cat and dog will often get on, with the cat taking charge from the start. This will not be true of a very dominant dog and a very nervous cat, but careful introductions should smooth out a pecking order.

Step 1: Swapping scents

First exchange scents in the same way that you do with two cats (see page 47). Once your cat and dog seem to be used to the smell of each other, move on to Step 2.

Step 2: Face to face

If your dog is excitable, take him for a long walk before this step to tire him out.

Keep your dog calm and put him on his lead before letting your cat into the same room. Sit with him in a corner of the room, away from the exit. This will help your cat feel calmer because he won't feel cornered. Allow your cat to come over: do not try to force him.

Result 1: The cat is interested and comes over. The dog remains calm. Reward them with some treats. If they seem unbothered by each other's presence, move to Step 3.
Result 2: The cat runs and the dog tries to chase. Hold your dog steady, return your cat to his safe room and repeat Step 2 later.

The swipe and the chase

Quite often a dog will approach a cat and the cat will greet this interest with a swipe of claws. This usually settles who is in charge and the dog will keep a respectful distance. However, a more nervous cat's instinct will be to run away. If you allow your dog to chase your cat, this can start a run-and-chase cycle – i.e. the dog will automatically chase the cat every time he sees him. This will be an incredibly difficult habit to break once it is established.

Step 3: Open introduction

When you think both your cat and dog are happy, you can remove the dog's lead – but only ever do this when your cat has an escape route and plenty of high places to jump to. Do not leave them together unsupervised until you are completely happy that your dog won't chase the cat.

For a kitten: A kitten is less able to defend himself, so take each stage very slowly and keep the kitten in his kitten cage until you are completely happy. Frequent and controlled meetings over a number of days should ensure a long and happy friendship.

Once all people and pets are introduced, you can move on to 'Exploring the new home'.

Exploring the new home

If you have introduced other pets, your new cat will already have experienced some of the other rooms in your house. Once he is happy with the other pets, he will continue to explore on his own. Make sure all windows, doors and cat flaps are closed, then just open the door to his safe room and let your new cat or kitten come out on his own.

For a cat: You don't have to watch him the entire time: he can make his own way around.
For a kitten: Kittens need close supervision, so don't just let him run around the house on his own. When no one is available to keep an eye on him, return him to his safe room.

It shouldn't take long for your cat to have a look around, but give him a month to get used to his new house before moving on to 'Going outside'.

GOING OUTSIDE

For a cat: An adult cat should not be allowed outside unless:
- He is confident around your house.
- He has been living in your house for at least four weeks.
- He has been microchipped or otherwise identified (see page 78).
- He (or she) has been neutered.
- He has been vaccinated.

It can be very tempting to let him out before these are all in place, but you should resist, even if he miaows at the door.

For a kitten: A kitten should not be allowed out unsupervised until he is at least six months old and **all** the above five points have been fulfilled.

When letting your cat or kitten out for the first time:
- Always do it just before dinner or breakfast. Expecting to be fed should prevent him from going too far and will make it easier to call him back.
- Open the door and allow your cat to choose whether he would like to go out. Do not pick him up and put him out because it will make him feel disorientated.
- Only leave him out for short periods of time at first, then gradually give him more freedom.
- Never force a cat to go out. If he is nervous, he may get scared and run away.

If your cat isn't keen on going out, you can try to encourage him by sitting in your garden so he can see you, playing with a toy or using treats so he follows you. Do not be concerned if your cat doesn't want to go outside – you should leave the decision up to him.

A Good Environment

Indoors or outdoors?

The most suitable environment for a cat is one that involves a mixture of indoor and outdoor living. Keeping cats shut indoors permanently is a contentious issue and one that causes many arguments between cat owners, breeders and vets. It is commonplace in the US and Australia, particularly with owners of pedigree cats, but in the UK it is widely considered to be the owner's responsibility to give a cat outside access.

Why Keep a Cat Permanently Indoors?

There are some circumstances which make it advisable to keep a cat permanently indoors. For example, a cat with a transferable disease such as Feline Immunodeficiency Virus (FIV) must be kept indoors to avoid him spreading FIV or catching another infection himself. Cats with disabilities such as deafness or blindness should also be kept indoors for their own safety, as they won't be able to avoid hazards such as dogs and cars. A few pedigree breeds are also not suited to an outdoor life, particularly those without a thick enough layer of protective fur. Even without these special cases to consider, some people prefer to keep cats indoors all the time because they do not want to expose them to outdoor hazards (see page 54).

Feral cats

Feral cats live in wild colonies in towns, cities or the countryside with very little or no contact with human beings. A domestic cat will not suddenly become feral if he is abandoned by his owner to find his own way in the world because he will still be used to living with humans; in this situation he would be considered a stray. If a stray cat has a litter of kittens and they grow up without being socialized with humans they will be feral. Feral cats are 'kept' by farmers, stable owners and smallholders as mousers. Most of these people feed the cats and give them veterinary treatment, such as neutering or vaccinations, but this would be done using a trap to catch the cat because a truly feral cat will not be handled easily. They have a bond to their territory and will remain in the area for as long as it proves valuable to them.

Advantages of an indoor life:

- Less hunting.
- Better relations with neighbours – some people dislike having cats in their gardens, especially if the garden is being used as a toilet.
- Less chance of fleas or ticks being picked up, unless you have other pets that go outside.
- Little chance of picking up infectious diseases or injuries through fighting with other cats.
- Little chance of going missing or being involved in a road traffic accident.
- Less chance of being poisoned – on purpose or by accident – by slug pellets, antifreeze or other outdoor chemicals.
- A longer average lifespan.

Disadvantages of an indoor life:

- Behaviour problems – a lack of mental stimulation may cause frustration and boredom which can lead to aggression, spraying or scratching problems. These can be expensive in terms of damaged furniture.
- Health problems – higher risk of feline obesity and the disorders associated with it.
- Lack of exercise and ability to act out natural instincts – e.g. hunting, scratching and scent marking.
- More chance of being poisoned by household chemicals, plants or medication.
- Lack of social development – e.g. over-dependence on human companions, an inability to interact with other cats and an excessive fear of the outside world.
- The inconvenience of cleaning out cat litter and having to keep all doors and windows closed.
- Any escape will be much more serious because your cat will not have any experience of the outside world.

Ultimately, you must decide what is best for you and your cat. You may find that keeping him permanently inside leads to some of the above problems, but you may also find that, though you give your cat free access to the outdoors, he seldom puts a paw through the cat flap.

See also 'The best of both worlds', page 55.

Life indoors

THE PERFECT INDOOR SPACE

From your cat's point of view the perfect indoor space is one that has plenty of things to keep his interest, is safe and provides for his needs. If you do not intend to allow your cat access to the outside world it is vital that you pay close attention to his indoor space as it will be his whole world.

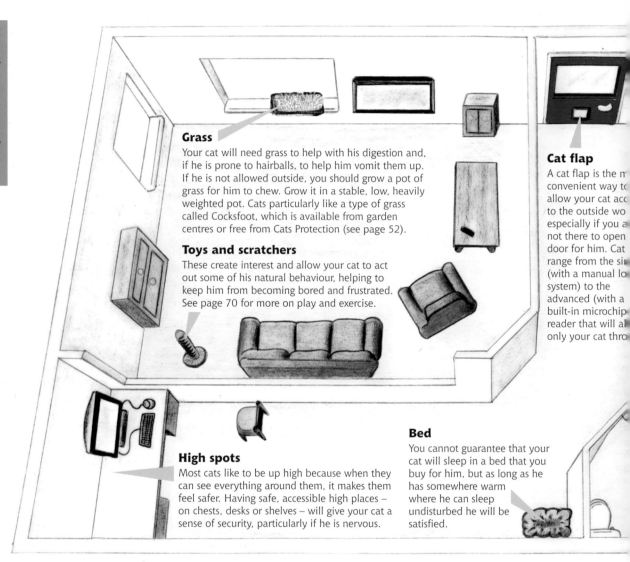

Grass

Your cat will need grass to help with his digestion and, if he is prone to hairballs, to help him vomit them up. If he is not allowed outside, you should grow a pot of grass for him to chew. Grow it in a stable, low, heavily weighted pot. Cats particularly like a type of grass called Cocksfoot, which is available from garden centres or free from Cats Protection (see page 52).

Toys and scratchers

These create interest and allow your cat to act out some of his natural behaviour, helping to keep him from becoming bored and frustrated. See page 70 for more on play and exercise.

Cat flap

A cat flap is the most convenient way to allow your cat access to the outside world especially if you are not there to open the door for him. Cat flaps range from the simple (with a manual locking system) to the advanced (with a built-in microchip reader that will allow only your cat through).

High spots

Most cats like to be up high because when they can see everything around them, it makes them feel safer. Having safe, accessible high places – on chests, desks or shelves – will give your cat a sense of security, particularly if he is nervous.

Bed

You cannot guarantee that your cat will sleep in a bed that you buy for him, but as long as he has somewhere warm where he can sleep undisturbed he will be satisfied.

INDOOR HAZARDS

It is particularly important for owners of indoor-only cats to watch for hazards. Cats kept indoors release their pent-up energy and curiosity on the world around them and, more than cats who go outside, they are inclined to chew, scratch and climb inappropriate objects.

Cupboards

Curiosity is a famous cat trait and if you leave a cupboard open for a while you may find that your cat sneaks in. Be particularly careful of warm airing cupboards – always check your cat isn't catching forty winks inside before you close the door, as being shut in a small warm space may cause him to overheat or become dehydrated.

High open windows or balconies

Despite their expert balance, a bad fall can cause a cat serious harm. It is possible to buy screens for open windows so that you and your cat can get the benefits of fresh air safely.

The elements

If your cat is not allowed outside, do make sure he gets plenty of opportunity to bask in sunshine, cool off in the shade and breathe fresh air.

Bowls

Clean bowls with fresh water and food should be made available to your cat. For more on food and water, see page 56.

Litter tray

Always have a clean litter tray and fresh litter for your cat to use as a toilet. For more on toileting, see page 64.

You

Cats have a habit of silently getting under your feet, which can be dangerous for both you and your cat.

Be especially careful when you are coming down the stairs, particularly if you are carrying something in front of you. You may not see your cat if he is curled up on a step, or if he suddenly stops where you are about to tread.

Watch out in the kitchen too. Tripping over your cat could cause a nasty accident if, for example, it makes you spill hot liquid or fat.

Christmas

Christmas trees, trailing lights and baubles can all seem like harmless playthings to your cat, but a falling tree, chewed wires and broken baubles all pose hazards. Also watch out for pine needles in paws and turkey bones being gulped down by a greedy cat. An older cat may take no notice of what's going on around him at this time of year, but younger and more curious cats can get into all sorts of trouble.

Also, don't forget that a nervous cat will find parties and crackers quite terrifying. You can buy crackers with the 'bang' removed if your pet is extremely nervous, but most will be happy enough if you just provide them with a quiet room away from all the noise.

Poisons

Cats are very susceptible to poisons, so it is fortunate that they have evolved to be picky about what they will swallow. Flea treatments meant for dogs and paracetamol are particularly poisonous to cats, but are sometimes administered by owners who are unaware of this. Bleach and other cleaning products are also toxic and can easily get on to cats' paws if newly cleaned surfaces are not kept closed off until they are completely dry.

For more on poisons, see page 54.

Plants

Cats rarely eat enough of things that are bad for them to suffer problems, but some plants and cut flowers do contain substances that are poisonous. It is a good idea to keep all houseplants and flowers out of reach. Indoor-only cats are more likely to chew pot plants and cut flowers, particularly if they are not given the opportunity to eat cat grass or are under-stimulated.

Lilies

All parts of the lily pose a threat to cats, but the pollen is particularly dangerous because if a cat knocks into a vase of flowers and the pollen falls on to his fur, he will groom it off later. Cats that ingest lily pollen can very quickly suffer kidney failure and die, so avoid these flowers if possible or, if you must have them, cut off the stamens and put the vase far out of reach.

In the UK, around 85 cats a year are poisoned by lilies.

Life outdoors

THE PERFECT OUTDOOR SPACE

Cats are happy to go out into any garden, but if you want to ensure that you, your cat and your neighbours live in harmony, then the following advice will help.

A private toilet

This is an excellent way of preventing your cat from using a neighbour's garden or an unsuitable area in your own. For information on creating a toilet area and encouraging your cat to use it, see page 66.

Shelter

Your cat may love to bask in the sunshine, but do make sure that there are plenty of shady spots to rest in. Cats, particularly white or pale cats, are prone to skin cancer, so keep an eye on any sun worshippers. If you think your cat is getting too much sun, you can bring him in at the hottest time of the day – between 11.30 a.m. and 2 p.m. – or you can use a sunblock on his ears and nose (any kind will do, though if your cat has sensitive skin it is best to use a baby sunblock).

Plants

Cats enjoy all sorts of plants, especial[l] when they can hide in amongst them, b[u] there are some that can present a danger: s[ee] 'Outdoor Hazards', page 54.

Cocksfoot grass It is good to plant an area of grass in your garden. Not only is this fun for your cat to hide in, but eating grass is vital for healthy digestion and – if your cat is susceptible to them – for getting rid of hairballs. Your cat will prefer Cocksfoot grass (available in garden centres or free from Cats Protecti[on] because it is long and broad-leaved so it is easy to che[w].

Catnip or catmint (*Nepeta cataria*) is a favourite of m[ost] although not all, cats. It produces oil that sends about [80?] per cent of cats into a state of extreme happiness, ma[king] them roll about and play in it. See box, page 71.

Safe places

Your cat will prefer his garden if there are some trees to climb or a garden s[eat to] sit on and watch the world go by. This will make him feel at ease in his terri[tory.]

52

Boundaries

It is very difficult to prevent a determined cat escaping from a garden, but it will appease any upset neighbours if they can see that you are trying. The following suggestions should help:

- Make your own garden as appealing as possible using the advice on these pages.
- Use 2-metre, close-boarded fencing around the border of your garden, or use one of the special types of fencing described in the box below.
- Plant a high hedge or climbing plant in front of the fence to prevent your cat from scaling it.

Territory marking

It is a cat's natural behaviour to spray urine or scratch upright objects to mark his territory. He is most likely to do this in areas that are prominent in the garden, such as corners that stick out or gateways and entrances. Here are some easy ways to reduce the impact on your garden:

- Get your cat neutered – neutered cats are less territorial.
- Help your cat feel safe – if he feels unsafe in his garden (e.g. if the neighbour's dog is constantly staring at him or if the garden is very open with nowhere to hide) then he will scent mark to make himself feel secure.
- Plant hardy shrubs and trees in key areas, including any protruding corners or at entrances to the garden.
- Provide solid, wooden posts for scratching – fence panels and sturdy tree trunks are ideal.

Deterrents

You can stop your cat from going into certain areas of your own or your neighbour's garden by trying some of the following:

- Plant closely to reduce access to bare soil for toileting.
- Use stone chippings, prickly plants, rocks or netting to cover bare soil and stop your cat from walking in a particular area.
- Spread citrus peel, 'Silent Roar' (lion-dung pellets) or chicken-manure pellets on any area into which you don't want your cat to go – he will dislike the smell and avoid these places.
- A water pistol sprayed near the cat, or an automatic water spray set off by an infra-red signal will show the cat that this is a no-go area.

er

cats prefer to drink
ater rather than tap
, so if you can provide
bowls in the garden
ideal. Ponds make
drinking spots, but keeping
a cat's garden can be a
er. If you want to keep
cover the pond with
g or surround it with
thing unpleasant like thick
or stone chippings to deter
cat from going near it.

Fencing your garden

The cat fence

You can buy fencing with a bend in the upper sections, making it impossible for a cat to climb over. It is usually made of a strong, netted material that is almost invisible and is safe for cats because they can't get tied up in it.

Rolling bars

This is a 'rolling pin'-style attachment that fixes to the top of your existing garden fence. The wooden rolling pin spins when the cat tries to grip it, with the result that he cannot get on to the top of the fence and has to jump down again.

The invisible fence

This is a controversial method involving a wire placed round the perimeter of the garden and a special collar that is worn by your cat. As he gets near the perimeter, the cat is warned by a beep before receiving a low-level electric shock. The idea is that your cat will learn to obey the beep and retreat before he gets the shock. Understandably, many cat owners and animal welfare charities consider this system inhumane.

OUTDOOR HAZARDS

Just as it is impossible for a human to avoid all the risks of going outside, so it is for your cat.

Wandering and getting lost

You can reduce the risk of your cat wandering off by:

- Keeping him in from dusk until dawn when he is less visible and more likely to wander further from home in order to hunt.
- Neutering your cat to reduce wandering, mating and territorial behaviour.
- Identifying your cat in case he gets lost – a collar disc with your phone number will enable anyone who finds him to contact you, and microchipping him will ensure that, if his collar is lost or removed, a vet, the police or an animal welfare charity will be able to trace you. If your cat wears a collar, use a quick-release safety type so that he won't get hooked up and stuck on anything.
- Ensuring that your garden is a fun and inviting place for your cat so he feels less inclined to wander elsewhere.

Cats rarely go missing without cause, unless they have not been neutered and are 'wandering' in search of a mate. Fireworks or storms could scare a cat into running away, while getting trapped in a vehicle might result in a cat being driven far from home. Always check sheds and garages before looking further afield. For more information on finding a lost cat, see page 79.

Plants

Many plants are potentially poisonous but it is very rare for a cat to eat enough of a poisonous plant to suffer any severe ill effects. As a general rule, any plant in a garden centre marked as toxic or irritating to humans will pose the same dangers to your cat, so it is best to position them in an area tightly packed with plants and well away from pathways from which they can be easily reached.

For a full list of potentially poisonous plants, contact the Feline Advisory Bureau (FAB). See also 'Lilies', page 51.

Poisons

Weedkiller, antifreeze, creosote and some slug pellets are poisonous to cats. As with poisonous plants, cats don't tend to eat things that are bad for them, but antifreeze is a particular danger because it does not have a scent that warns cats of its poisonous nature.

Road traffic accidents

Many cats are killed on the roads each year. There is some debate over whether living near a busy road increases this danger: it has been suggested recently that cats living in such areas are more road-aware and so are less at risk.

Dogs, people and other cats

Even a neutered cat may have a confrontation with another cat from time to time, although cats are rarely hurt seriously in these scuffles. Sometimes cats can contract infectious diseases – such as feline leukaemia,

What goes up in a flash doesn't always come down so easily.

FIV and cat flu – from each other when they fight so it is important to keep your cat's vaccinations up to date.

Dogs and people can pose a greater risk, but cases where a dog is allowed to pursue a cat in the open or where people persecute cats are thankfully quite rare.

Trees

Cats are great climbers when they are going up, but getting down is a different matter. Their claws curve in only one direction so, to get down again, most cats have to climb down backwards – an undignified manoeuvre which they don't much like.

If your cat gets stuck up a tree, try to coax him down with some food or use a ladder to get to him. If this fails and you need help, the RSPCA is the only organization authorized to call out the fire brigade to rescue a cat.

Fleas, worms and ticks

Being outside does expose your cat to certain parasites, but proper preventative treatment will help protect him. See page 84, for more information.

Hunting

Although not technically a hazard, the cat's instinct to hunt can be quite distasteful to cat owners and can sometimes bring them into confrontation with neighbours – particularly birdwatchers.

Recent studies show that wild birds make up a relatively small proportion of cats' prey in the UK (about 20 per cent) and some cats can barely muster enough energy to catch a worm, let alone a bird. That said, if your cat is a hunter and you want to share your garden with both him and the local wildlife, here are a few simple steps you can take:

- Fit your cat with a quick-release collar and bell, so that birds can hear him coming.
- Put bird feeders up high on posts and away from possible pouncing platforms.
- Surround the base of bird feeders with prickly plants or a cat deterrent.
- Encourage more birds into your garden. Studies show that the more birds there are in a garden the less chance there is of one of them being surprised by a cat.
- Give your cat plenty of opportunity to practise his hunting instincts at home by playing games with him.
- Keep him inside at night, during dawn and dusk when cats most like to hunt.
- Plant prickly shrubs like holly to give birds somewhere to sit and nest unharassed.

Having been prized throughout history for keeping rat and mice infestations from our doors, cats still target rodents more than any other creature.

Walking your cat

One way in which you can give your cat restricted access to the outdoors is to walk him on a harness and lead around your garden. A cat that has been taught from an early age to wear a harness will be quite content to walk like this. However, it will be difficult to teach an adult cat who has never worn one to do so at ease, and it is not the ideal solution for an animal as naturally acrobatic and free-spirited as a cat.

If you want to introduce your kitten to the harness and lead, first put the harness on and let him get used to wearing it around the house for a few days. Make sure he is comfortable with the harness before attaching the lead inside your house. Do not try to walk your cat outside until you are sure he will not panic, and don't forget to make sure your cat is suitably identified in case of escape (see page 78 for more information on identification).

This cat is obviously quite happy to be walked on a lead.

The best of both worlds

If you want to combine the safety of indoors and some of the stimulation of the outside world, then restricted outdoor access – where you create an outdoor run for your cat – may be a good solution. However, this option is quite expensive and will take up a large section of your outside space.

Similar to a rabbit run but on a much larger scale, this kind of system can be as grand or as simple as you like. The best are either attached (like an extension) to the side or back of the house and accessed via a cat flap, or are separate from the house but are attached via a walkway that stretches from a cat flap to the run. Others are completely separate from the house but are not as practical for you or your cat because you will have to take him to and from the enclosure. If it is separate you must remember to provide all the essential items listed below and also access to a fresh supply of water, because he will not be able to choose to come inside when he wants to.

How much space?

How big you make your cat run depends on how much space you have to start with and how many cats you intend to put in it. It is advisable to make it at least 2.5–3 metres square and around 2 metres high but, as a rule, the larger the run the better.

Building your run

Most cat runs are made from a wooden frame and chicken wire, but as long as the structure is completely secure you can make it out of any suitable outdoor building material. If you are not very practical when it comes to DIY, try a local handyman, fencing specialist, landscape gardener or builder. There are also pre-made cat runs available that look similar to a shed or summerhouse; these can be purchased on the internet.

Essentials for your run

To make an outside environment enriching and safe you should include:

- Climbing facilities – a small tree or two included within the run or some very stable man-made climbing frames.
- Shelter – plants and/or man-made shelters that protect from the sun, wind and rain are essential.
- High platforms – a tree's branches, or platforms attached to a post, will give your cat plenty of places to perch and watch the world go by.
- Grass – it is a great idea to grow a section of cat grass, as your cat can play in it and eat it as well (see pages 50 and 52).
- Toilet area – keep a well-dug area of soil as far away as possible from the rest of the facilities so your cat can use it as a toilet.

If you want to make the run somewhere nice for both you and your cat to spend time, include a bench, table and chairs or lounger so you can sit outside with him.

FEEDING YOUR CAT

Providing your cat with the correct nutritional balance is vital in preventing illness and expensive trips to the vet.

The correct diet

Food must contain the correct protein, fat, carbohydrate, mineral and vitamin balance, as illustrated below, to provide energy and nourishment, and to prevent illness.

Your cat needs meat

In the wild, cats live on a diet consisting wholly of small animals. Taken together, the skin, bones, flesh, fur and organs of their prey give them everything they need to survive. In fact, your cat is an 'obligate carnivore', which means that he must eat other animals in order to get the nutrients he needs.

No need for supplements

If your cat has a balanced diet he will not need nutritional supplements unless a vet prescribes them. Excess nutrients can be as damaging as a lack of them.

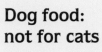

Cats have to eat meat to survive.

Dog food: not for cats

Although cats and dogs are both often referred to as carnivores, in fact a dog is an omnivore – meaning that he eats both animal and vegetable matter and his dietary needs are quite different. Your cat needs twice as much protein as a dog, and needs 41 essential nutrients to maintain health, whereas a dog needs only 37. For this reason, cat and dog foods are made with different nutrient levels and a cat fed on dog food will not be able to function properly.

Protein is found in meat, fish and eggs and provides the amino acids vital for chemical processes to take place in the body. Cats are unable to manufacture the amino acids taurine and arginine. Taurine is found only in meat, and a deficiency can cause blindness, heart disease and death.

Vitamins, such as A, D and B2, are found in liver, dairy and plant products and are used in many of the cat's vital bodily functions, from metabolism to vision. A lack of vitamin A can result in blindness, while too much can lead to spinal defects. Cats are unable to make vitamin D but can, unlike humans, make their own vitamin C so they don't need extra in their diet.

Minerals, such as calcium, iron and potassium, are found in bone, meat, dairy products and vegetables. Deficiencies can cause infertility, weight loss, growth problems, heart and nervous system disorders. Excesses can cause kidney and urinary tract disorders and high blood pressure.

Water is essential because about 67 per cent of your cat's total body weight is water and it must be kept hydrated. Water also flushes out toxins in the kidneys.

Carbohydrate is found in plants and dairy products, and provides energy and fibre.

Fat is found in animal fat, fish oil and vegetable oil; it provides fatty acids vital for the brain and for energy. Cats are unable to make their own linoleic and arachidonic acids. Arachidonic acid is found only in animal fat.

Types of food

The simplest and most convenient way to feed a cat is with a pre-prepared cat food and fresh water. The alternative is home-made food, though this method is more time consuming and requires careful research to ensure that you are creating a safe and balanced diet.

PRE-PREPARED FOOD

Commercial food is nutritionally balanced and convenient. Cat foods are classified as either 'complete' or 'complementary' and manufacturers must state clearly on the packet which their food is.

Complete foods, which come in either wet or dry forms (see below), contain the whole range of nutrients needed for a balanced diet. A cat does not need any additional food.

Complementary foods alone do **not** provide a daily ration of nutrients and so must be given only in addition to another food. Cat treats fall into this category.

Wet food

Wet food comes in tins or pouches in a wide range of flavours. It is similar in texture to a fresh meat diet.

Advantages. It comes in ready-made portions and is often more appetizing to a fussy cat.

Disadvantages. If left out in warm weather, it becomes stale and attracts flies. It is more expensive than dry food.

Dry food

The greater the quantity you buy, the better value it is. The biscuits or 'kibble' comes in different shapes and sizes.

Advantages. It is more cost-effective than wet food and practical as it can be left out without becoming inedible.

Disadvantages. The lack of moisture may be unsuitable for some cats, particularly if they suffer from urinary problems. Flavour choice is more limited.

A combination of wet and dry food, offering the benefits of both and some variety, may be the best option.

ALTERNATIVE FOODS

Some people choose to feed their cat a home-made diet or raw food. If you are interested in these methods, seek advice from your vet and research the nutritional needs of cats carefully. It is only advisable to give these foods if you have the time and knowledge to do so correctly.

Home-made food can be prepared from a combination of poultry, meat, fish, eggs and certain vegetables. It is recommended that you cook any animal products because, like humans, cats can become ill from eating bacteria found in some uncooked derivatives. Bones are useful for cleaning teeth but care should be taken with them, particularly if your cat is likely to gulp his food down.

BARF, or Biologically Appropriate Raw Food, is a method of feeding based on the idea that cats and dogs should only be fed uncooked bones and meat, as they would get in the wild. It is a controversial form of feeding because of the higher risk of food poisoning and choking that is associated with uncooked meat and bones. Some pet-food manufacturers have already developed 'convenient' raw food diets that can be kept in a freezer until needed.

CHANGING YOUR CAT'S FOOD

If you want to change your cat's food from one type to another, it is advisable to do so gradually by mixing in small portions of the new food with his normal food and increasing it over time. Getting your cat used to different foods and flavours from an early age will make him less susceptible to stomach upsets and will make introducing new foods or changing foods easier.

Treats

It is always nice to treat your cat, but too many treats can lead to obesity and illness so keep them to a minimum.

Pre-prepared treats. Commercial cat treats come in hundreds of different forms, from chicken-flavoured biscuits to freeze-dried shrimps. Some have 'added extras' like dental, breath-freshening or hairball-control benefits.

Home-made treats. Cats often like a little bit of tuna, but if it is preserved in brine it will have a very high salt content; use fresh tuna or tuna in spring water. Most cats love liver, but it contains lots of vitamin A, an excess of which can be toxic: offer it only once a week at most.

Foods to avoid

Unless you know it is safe, always avoid giving your cat 'human' food, and in particular ensure he doesn't eat:

Chocolate contains caffeine which can affect the heart and nervous system.

Onions and garlic cause anaemia.

Grapes or raisins can damage the kidneys.

Tomatoes/green potatoes can cause a stomach upset.

Understanding food labels

Pet-food labels can be quite confusing, but it is possible to get most of the information you need if you know how to interpret them.

All pet foods must be labelled as 'complete' or 'complementary' and state which species the food is for.

All pet food must display directions for use.

The list of ingredients states where the nutritional content comes from. It is listed in descending order by weight and can be indicated by category names (e.g. meat and animal derivatives) or by individual names (e.g. chicken). If the food has a particular flavour, such as chicken, then that ingredient must be named individually in the ingredients list (e.g. chicken – minimum 4 per cent).

Any added preservatives, antioxidants, colourants or vitamins A, D and E have to be stated.

The name and address of the manufacturer must be given on the packaging.

Some cat foods include words like 'premium' and 'deluxe' but these terms don't actually mean anything and should be ignored.

This is the nutritional content of the food. The percentage of protein, oil and fats, fibre, moisture (if over 14 per cent) and mineral content (called 'ash') must be stated.

The batch number (or a date of manufacture) must be given so that the product's origin can be traced. This often appears near the 'best before' date.

Pusscat
Fisherman's Choice

PETFOOD INC.

THE COMPLETE FOOD FOR YOUR CAT

FEEDING GUIDELINES:
Individual needs vary.
Fresh, clean water should always be available.
The following is based on a moderately active adult cat:

Cat Weight:	Feed per day
3kg	55g
4kg	75g
5kg	90g

INGREDIENTS:
Cereals, fish and fish derivatives (min 4% fish), vegetable protein extracts, oils and fats, derivatives of vegetable origin, minerals, vegetables, milk and milk derivatives, yeasts. Coloured with and preserved with EC additives.

VITAMINS:
Vitamin A:	8500 IU/kg
Vitamin B₃:	850 IU/kg
Vitamin E:	75mg/kg
Taurine:	1000mg/kg

TYPICAL ANALYSIS:
Protein	32%
Fat	10%
Ash	8%
Fibre	3%
Calcium	1.3%
Phosphorus	1.2%
Potassium	0.7%
Magnesium	0.1%
Methionine	0.6%
Copper*	19mg/kg

* (as copper sulphate):

Vitamin levels are guaranteed up to best before date.
For best before date, batch and registration number see box.
The product should be stored in a dry and clean place at ambient temperature.

Net Weight: 900g

Address all enquiries to:
Petfood Inc., PO Box 123, Catford, London, CA20 1BC

Best before:
07.08.09
48395500005 09:21

Specialist food

Pregnancy, nursing mothers and kittens Kitten food is very rich and is used not only to feed kittens but also pregnant cats (in their last two to three weeks) and nursing mothers to give the extra energy and nutrients they need to support growth.

Senior As your cat gets older – after the age of eight – he may become less active, have difficulty digesting carbohydrates and be more prone to certain diseases. Senior food is carefully balanced to counter the effects of age and help maintain health.

Mother cats need extra energy to produce milk.

Other special diets There is a huge number of special diets on the market, including:
• Dental diets with larger, stronger kibble size to help scrape plaque from the teeth and maintain a healthy mouth.
• Light diets with reduced calories for overweight cats.
• Hairball-control diets to reduce hairballs collecting in the stomach.
• Sensitive diets for cats with sensitive stomachs.

Organic food is not necessarily better nutritionally for your cat, but it may be better for the environment.

These kittens need to be fed a special diet so that they have all the nutrients they need for growth.

WHICH FOOD IS BEST?

Choosing between all the different foods can be tricky, not least because no one agrees on what is the best kind of food for cats. However, there are a few ways you can gauge the quality of cat food.

Cost

Price is a good indicator. As a general rule, very cheap pet food contains lower quality proteins and fats which are harder to digest.

Comparison with other foods

Foods contain different quantities of moisture, so to compare their nutritional value you need to calculate the dry matter of the food. For example.

Food A is a wet food with 8% protein and 80% moisture.
Food B is a dry food with 32% protein and 8% moisture.

At first glance, food B looks like a much better option because of its high protein content, but to find the actual protein value you need to do this equation:

$$\text{Protein value} = \frac{\text{Protein content} \times 100}{\text{Dry matter content}}$$

Dry matter content is 100 minus moisture content. An easy calculation with wet food, but with dry foods the moisture content is rarely stated on the label. They contain between 6 per cent and 10 per cent moisture and it has to be declared only if it exceeds 14 per cent. Use the average of 8 per cent – ring the manufacturer if you want an exact figure.

Food A	Food B
Protein value: $\dfrac{8 \times 100}{20} = 40\%$	Protein value: $\dfrac{32 \times 100}{92} = 35\%$

Meat proteins versus wheat proteins

Protein can come from many sources, including wheat. A food may have a high protein content but it may be made up of a large proportion of wheat products. It is meat that your cat needs, so look for meat products near the top of the ingredients list (remember they are listed in order of weight) and watch out for lots of small wheat products adding up to a larger overall wheat content. As a rule, the simpler the ingredients list the purer the cat food.

How much food and how often?

There are no fixed rules for feeding because each cat is different. The easiest way is to follow the manufacturer's guidelines and then adjust the amount and the frequency to suit your cat.

HOW MUCH?

The quantity of food your cat eats depends on his weight. Check this on a routine trip to the vet or weigh your cat at home. To do this, pick him up, stand on the scales and note the result. Weigh yourself and subtract this from the first result. This is your cat's weight.

Once you know his weight you can use the guidelines on the food packet to work out how much he needs.

Wet food

Packets normally say how many pouches or tins the 'average' cat (weighing about 4 kg) needs per day.

Dry food

The packet will tell you how much food a cat of a given weight will need each day. If your cat is 3.8 kg, the closest weight listed may be 4 kg, so you should give the daily amount recommended for that weight.

To avoid having to weigh food each day, you could weigh it once and then see how many spoonfuls it comes to. You can then measure out the appropriate amount each day using the spoon as a guide.

Don't double feed

If you are feeding a mix of wet and dry food, don't forget to halve the recommended amounts of each, or you will be feeding your cat two daily portions.

What else affects quantity?

A number of things besides weight determine the amount of food a cat needs:

- Age – cats' energy needs usually reduce with age.
- Food – some foods are much higher in energy and nutrients than others.
- Activity – an active cat will need more food than an inactive one.
- Metabolism – like humans, some cats naturally use up energy faster than others and so need extra food to compensate.

HOW OFTEN?

You can give your cat the entire day's portion in one meal, though as a rule cats prefer smaller, more frequent meals so it is often best to give two or three small meals spread throughout the day. This may not be possible if you are out at work, so one or two larger meals may be the solution.

Some people give their cat a constant supply of dry food to nibble at all day. This is called free-feeding and can easily lead to obesity if your cat is unable to regulate his own intake. Leaving wet food out all day is not recommended, as it can go off, so free-feeding is suitable only for a dry-food diet.

PREGNANCY AND KITTENS

Pregnant cats, nursing cats and kittens all need more energy and nutrients each day than a normal adult cat.

Pregnant cats need to eat about 50 per cent more than usual. When the kittens are born, the mother's food needs increase dramatically. At this point the mother should be free-fed good-quality, high-energy kitten food.

For approximately the first five weeks kittens feed entirely on their mother's milk which is high in fat and protein. From weaning until around six months old kittens need good-quality kitten food at least four times a day. They must be fed regularly because they have very small stomachs and cannot eat large meals. From six months to one year old, this can be reduced to three meals a day. After one year, kittens are classed as adults and can eat a normal adult diet.

ALWAYS MONITOR PROGRESS

Keep an eye on your cat to see whether he is maintaining, gaining or losing weight and make adjustments as necessary. For more on weight problems, see 'Eating problems', page 61.

A wild diet

An adult cat living in the wild would need about five whole mice (about 140 g total) per day to survive.

Drinking

The only drink your cat needs is water – it is the most important nutrient you can give him. Although he can lose most of his fat and half his protein and still survive, it takes only a 10 per cent loss of water for a cat to become seriously ill.

All you need to give is tap water. He should always have a fresh, clean supply available in a bowl, but don't be surprised if you don't see him drink from it very often: many cats prefer to find their water elsewhere, such as in puddles and ponds.

The amount your cat drinks will be affected by his diet. A cat fed entirely on wet food (about 80 per cent water) may need very little extra water because he will get almost all he needs from his food. A cat fed on a dry diet (8 per cent water) will need to drink extra water to meet his needs.

AVOID MILK AND CREAM

Your cat may like cow's milk or cream but he doesn't need them, and the lactose in them may cause stomach upsets. Specialist cat and kitten milks with a reduced lactose content are available; these can be given as a treat but should not be used to replace water.

Eating problems

By far the most common eating problem in cats is obesity, but cats can also under-eat and become anorexic. While obesity and anorexia tend to happen over time, if your cat shows sudden and rapid change in weight or appetite you should take him to the vet, as these can be signs of other serious illnesses.

WHAT IS A HEALTHY WEIGHT?

Like people, cats come in different shapes and sizes. A 'big-boned' or large cat may be a healthy 6 kg. A much smaller, petite cat may be only 3 kg. Neither is unhealthy. The best way to judge if your cat is the right weight is by sight. Ask your vet if you are unsure.

Obese
From the top: look for a triangular shape with much wider hind end than shoulders.
From the side: look out for a sagging stomach that makes the legs look unusually short.
Feel: for a flabby stomach and a layer of thick fat over the ribs and hips.

Healthy
From the top: look for a rectangle with a defined dip at the hips.
From the side: leg shape should be clearly visible and the chest should be deep, going back to a shallower waist.
Feel: for a soft, muscular body and a light layer of fat over the ribs.

Underweight
From the top: look for ribs and hips sticking out.
From the side: ribcage will be visible with a severe angle up to the waist.
Feel: for protruding bones and lack of fat over the ribs.

This cat's health could suffer because of his weight.

This cat is being hand fed because he has stopped eating.

UNDERWEIGHT CATS

If your cat is underweight but eats everything you give him, increase his food a little and see if he puts on weight.

If your cat is not eating what you give him, it may be because he is fussy, stressed or ill.

Encourage him to eat more by trying different flavours and types of food, giving smaller portions more regularly, and warming his wet food slightly to release the smell. A stronger flavour, such as fish, or hand-feeding may help.

OVERWEIGHT CATS

About 25 per cent of cats in the UK and 40 per cent in the US are obese. Obese cats have a poor quality of life because they are unable to run, jump and climb like other cats. They are also prone to weight-related illnesses such as heart disease, diabetes, arthritis, skin problems and premature death.

Usually cats become obese for one of three reasons: because they are fed too much, because they get too little exercise, or because they are being fed by more than one person.

Overeating

If your cat is free-fed or is given treats, this may be the cause of the problem. Switch him to a regulated diet and stop giving treats.

If he is already on a regulated diet, try reducing the amount of food he is allowed. This must be done gradually. Never crash-diet your cat, as this can cause liver problems. Alternatively, swap him to a specialist lower-calorie food and follow the instructions on the packet. If you are not comfortable planning your cat's reduced diet, you can visit your vet who will be happy to help.

Lack of exercise

Without exercise, your cat won't use up his recommended daily amount of calories. Playing, scratching, climbing and being outside all help burn up calories. For tips on exercising your cat, see 'Sleep, Play and Exercise', page 70.

Eating out

If you know someone else is feeding your cat, politely ask them to stop. You can also buy a quick-release collar with a personalized printed message reading 'Please do not feed me'.

SUDDEN CHANGES IN EATING OR DRINKING

Changes in your cat's eating or drinking habits can be a sign of illness, such as hyperthyroidism or diabetes, so it is important to keep an eye out for them. Take your cat to the vet if:

- He has not eaten for 48 hours.
- He suddenly seems constantly hungry.
- He loses weight without reason.
- He starts drinking a lot more than usual.

Feeding equipment

For feeding your cat, you need at least two bowls – one for food and one for water. You will want these bowls to remain still as the cat eats, so as to keep spills to a minimum, and to be safe and easy to clean. You will also need a spoon that is different from your other spoons to use for dishing out and cutting up food.

BOWLS

Bowls come in all different sizes, can be made of plastic, ceramic or steel and can be bought either separately or as a single unit, with the two bowls joined.

All-in-one food and water bowls are generally cheaper than two separate bowls but they are not ideal because your cat's water can become contaminated with food more easily.

Size

Bowls need to be wide and deep enough that food and water do not spill out, and so that your cat can easily reach the contents without having to squash his whiskers.

The best size for a food bowl is quite shallow – between 2.5 and 5 cm deep. The best size for a water bowl is between 5 and 8 cm deep. They should both be around 13 cm wide.

Material

Bowls should not move around as your cat eats, so they should either be heavy or have a rubber base to keep them stable. It is also important that they do not scratch easily because scratches allow bacteria and odour to settle, which could deter your cat from eating. If you want to wash the bowls in a dishwasher, make sure that they are dishwasher safe.

Plastic bowls are cheap and unbreakable but they tend to be very light and are not odour- or scratch-resistant. Some cats are allergic to plastic.

Steel bowls are more expensive than plastic bowls. They are quite lightweight but often come with a rubber base to keep them steady. Steel bowls are unbreakable, durable, hygienic and odour- and scratch-resistant.

Ceramic bowls are generally more expensive than either steel or plastic. They are heavy, hygienic and odour- and scratch-resistant, but they are breakable.

AUTOMATIC FEEDERS

These come in various different guises and (as long as your cat has free access to the outdoors) can be used for short periods while you are away. Dry food is placed in each compartment and a timer gives the cat access to food once or twice a day. It is not advisable to use wet food with an automatic feeder, as it can go off.

ON-DEMAND FEEDERS

These feeders release more food into a bowl as your cat eats. They should not be used with wet food.

Using this type of feeder means that you tend not to monitor closely what your cat is eating. This can be a problem for two reasons. First, many cats are unable to regulate their own food intake (see 'How much food and how often?', page 60); second, a change in your cat's eating habits is one of the first signs of serious illness (see page 62).

WATER FOUNTAINS

Water fountains use a pump to circulate water and dispense a constant stream into the bowl. Some cats prefer water delivered like this and will lap at the stream with their tongues. Water fountains have to be plugged in to the mains.

FEEDING MATS

Putting a washable mat under your cat's bowls makes it easier to pick up any spills and keeps the floor clean. You can buy rubber versions that help to keep bowls steady.

DRIED-FOOD CONTAINERS

An airtight container with a scoop or spoon is very useful for keeping dried food fresh.

Some cats prefer to drink running water.

TOILETING

One of the most common reasons for a cat to be unhappy is that his toileting arrangements are not right – from his point of view. Everything from the type of litter to the position of the toilet needs to be just right or you may find your cat relieving himself elsewhere.

Litter

Litter needs to be absorbent and loose but there are many differences between the types on offer. The main ones are:

MINERAL-BASED LITTERS

Clay – non-clumping
Price: Low.
Environmental: Clay is obtained via mining operations, which are environmentally costly. It is not biodegradable so will ultimately end up as landfill.
Cleanliness: Clay litters are dusty and so tend to get picked up by the cat's feet and spread around the floor and nearby carpets (called tracking).
Maintenance: High. Non-clumping clay litters need cleaning regularly because they do not contain the waste. Trays may need full cleaning more than once a week depending on the level of use.

Clay – clumping
Price: Moderate.
Environmental: Clay is obtained via mining operations, which are environmentally costly. It is not biodegradable so will ultimately end up as landfill.
Cleanliness: Clumping clay litters are both dusty and very easily tracked. Clumping occurs when the clay comes into contact with moisture, so cats can have clumped litter caught on their feet and in their fur around their back legs and bottom.
Maintenance: Moderate. Clumping litters keep the litter tray and surrounding litter cleaner because they contain the waste. They are easier to clean out because the waste forms into a lump that can be removed from the rest of the litter.

Silica – non-clumping
Price: High.
Environmental: Silica is obtained via mining operations, which are environmentally costly. It is not biodegradable so will ultimately end up as landfill.
Cleanliness: Silica litter creates no dust and very little tracking. It also contains an odour neutralizer to reduce smells, and urine is locked away inside the silica, helping to keep the tray clean.
Maintenance: Low. Faeces are removed when they are noticed but urine is not. The litter is stirred each day until the silica is completely saturated, then the whole tray is replaced.

PLANT-BASED LITTERS

Vegetable – clumping or non-clumping
Price: High.
Environmental: These litters are made from waste plant material, such as corn or wheat husks, so are better for the environment. They are biodegradable, so wet and discarded litter (but not the cat faeces) can be put on to a compost heap.
Cleanliness: Minimal dust and tracking occur, although some pellets may be kicked out of the tray. Non-clumping varieties can be flushed away (always read the packet carefully before flushing any litter).
Maintenance: Moderate to high. Clumping varieties make it easier to remove waste and help to keep the tray and surrounding litter cleaner.

Wood – non-clumping
Price: High.
Environmental: These litters are biodegradable and are made from waste sawdust. The wet and discarded litter (but not the cat faeces) can be put on to a compost heap.
Cleanliness: Minimal dust and tracking occur, although some pellets may be kicked out of the tray. The natural pine scent of some varieties helps to neutralize odours.
Maintenance: High. Non-clumping litters need cleaning regularly because they do not contain the waste. Trays may need full cleaning more than once a week depending on the level of use.

Paper – clumping
Price: Moderate.
Environmental: These litters are biodegradable and are made from recycled paper. The wet and discarded litter (but not the cat faeces) can be put on to a compost heap.
Cleanliness: There is no dust and very little tracking with this variety. Most can be flushed away.
Maintenance: High. These litters often clump when first wet, but if left to dry will break up. Trays may need full cleaning more than once a week depending on the level of use.

LITTER TRAYS AND ACCESSORIES

Once you have decided which litter you plan to use, you will need a tray to put it in and a scoop for removing waste. There are many different options, but which you use will depend on what your cat prefers. Other accessories are not essential but you may find them useful.

Trays

Standard. A plastic tray with sides, these are cost effective, simple to use and readily available. Some come with a rim that fits on the top to catch litter that is kicked up when your cat digs.

Hooded or covered. This is a standard tray with a cover that clips on top. These give complete privacy to your cat, contain all litter inside the tray and reduce the odours escaping. They are useful for keeping dogs and children out of the litter, but some cats are not comfortable in such an enclosed space. It is easy to forget to clean these trays, so you should be careful about carrying out regular checks.

Self-cleaning. Some 'self-cleaning' trays require that you lift a sieve or roll the litter tray to collect the clumped litter; others are fitted with fully automatic raking systems. These trays may provide some benefit for very picky cats or for owners who prefer to stay as far away from dirty litter as possible, but you still have to dispose of the soiled litter and clean the tray regularly and they are much more expensive than other trays.

Scoops

You can buy a solid scoop or one with holes in it. A solid scoop is best for use with litters that disintegrate when wet and a holed scoop is better for clumping types of litter so that unused litter can fall away.

Bags

You will need to dispose of the waste carefully. You can buy special bags but nappy bags will do just as well.

Liners

These can be plain or scented and they line the bottom of the tray so that when you come to clean it you simply remove the liner and all its contents. Some cats do not like the feel of the liner when they dig and scented varieties can smell too overpowering for the sensitive feline nose.

Mats

This can be a normal doormat or a special litter-tray mat placed under the tray to reduce tracking of litter throughout the house.

Your cat will help you choose

Cats can be quite picky about where they go to the toilet, so before you bring your new cat home ask the breeder or previous owner what type of litter tray and litter he has been using. To help with the transition of moving to a new environment, it is best to use the same type for the first few months while your cat settles in. If you want to change litter, do so by gradually mixing the new type in with the old and increasing the amount until you have completely swapped them over.

Toileting basics

Depending on his environment and character, your cat will go to the toilet outside in your garden, inside in a litter tray or a mixture of the two. There are a few rules that apply whether he goes to the toilet inside or outside.

Safety – cats feel vulnerable when going to the toilet and need their toilet area to be where they feel secure

Privacy – cats do not like to feel watched when they use the toilet

Digging material – cats like to bury their faeces so need a loose, dry substance to go to the toilet in

Cleanliness – your cat will be unwilling to use a dirty toilet area

GOING OUTSIDE

You will need a litter tray for at least the first month that you own your cat because he won't be able to go outside until he has settled in. After this, he may prefer always to go to the toilet outside.

Creating a toilet area in your garden is an excellent way of preventing your cat from using a neighbour's garden or an unsuitable area in your own. From your cat's point of view, the best toilet is:
- Made of well-dug, loose earth or fine bark.
- Sheltered and secluded – from the elements and from nosy neighbours.
- Clean – regularly dug over so the soiled areas can decompose.
- Large – around 100 cm x 50 cm will be enough, but the more space you can give, the cleaner the area will stay.

Encourage your cat

Your cat may abandon the litter tray as soon as he is allowed outside, but if he feels insecure he may prefer to continue using it. You cannot force your cat to use an outside toilet, but to encourage him mix some soiled cat litter from his tray into the earth so that it smells familiar to him.

Don't give up the litter tray

Even if your cat goes to the toilet outside all the time, there may be occasions when he wants to use a litter tray, e.g. when it is raining or if he feels unwell. If you can, it's best to keep a litter tray available at all times.

GOING INSIDE

In most cases cats find using a litter tray very straightforward and some prefer it to going outside.

By the time you bring a kitten home, he may have learnt how to use the litter tray from his mother. If not, it won't take long to show him what to do. After he has eaten, place him in his tray, wait for him to use it, then give him lots of praise. After only two or three attempts he should get the idea.

Position your cat's litter tray somewhere private and quiet. Try not to put it next to his feeding area or near a doorway, particularly a full glass one that looks out on to a garden as this will make him feel exposed and, if he is nervous, may put him off using the tray.

The one-plus-one rule

It is a good idea to provide one litter tray per cat plus one extra – especially for indoor-only cats. If you have more than one cat their litter trays should be placed in different locations – not in a row, as this may cause confrontations.

Cleanliness

Cats are very clean and do not like to use a dirty toilet. Read the instructions on the litter you choose to make sure that you are using enough. Scoop out soiled and wet litter as soon as you notice it and refill with fresh litter as necessary. At least once a week, wash the tray and completely change the litter.

THINGS CAN GO WRONG

Occasionally a cat may start to go to the toilet in the 'wrong' place. This is almost certainly a sign that something is not right, either with your cat or with the toilet arrangements you have made for him. See page 103.

This eight-week-old kitten has already learnt how to use his litter tray.

GROOMING

Although cats are very good at keeping themselves clean, part of owning a happy cat is looking after his skin, fur and claws through regular grooming. Lack of grooming can lead to dirty fur, stress and even painful matting.

Why groom?

Grooming not only keeps your cat's coat in good order but also gives you the opportunity to check for cuts, lumps or sore limbs. Brushing improves circulation and removes dead hairs to give his coat a healthy shine. And regular grooming will help to build a bond between you.

REDUCING HAIRBALLS

Your cat will regularly groom himself from head to tail, so it is likely – especially if he is longhaired – that at some point he will throw up a hairball.

To groom himself, he uses his rough tongue to tug at loose hairs in his coat. Usually these are ingested and passed out in the faeces, but if too many are swallowed they can collect into a ball in the cat's stomach and have to be vomited up. This may never happen or it may happen once in a while, but if you regularly groom your cat you will be helping to remove the dead hairs from his coat, which will reduce the chance of hairballs forming.

If your cat is regularly throwing up hairballs you should visit your vet because it may be a sign that there is a blockage in his digestive system.

REDUCING MATTING

Matting begins as a simple tangle in the fur but can rapidly get worse. Apart from not being very nice to look at, matted fur restricts your cat's movement by pulling at his skin. This can cause anything from slight discomfort to severe pain and open sores. Serious matting may have to be removed under anaesthetic by a vet, but you can avoid all that by regular grooming.

How often?

Regular grooming is important for your cat's health. How often you do it depends on:

• Texture and length of fur – very short, fine fur may need grooming only once a fortnight, but long, dense fur will need grooming as often as once a day.
• Activity and behaviour – if your cat is very active out of doors, he will pick up more tangles and plant matter in his fur than a lazy, indoor-only cat.
• Age – as your cat gets older, he may start to neglect his grooming and need extra help to keep clean and tidy.

START EARLY

An adult cat who has never been groomed may be unwilling to sit still while you do it. If you can, begin grooming when he is a kitten and get him used to having his feet touched and held. When you groom him and clip his claws later (see page 68) it will make the whole process much simpler.

This cat's long, thick fur means that he will need daily help from his owner with grooming.

How to groom

Groom your cat with a suitable brush or comb and at a quiet time of day when he is sleeping or resting after a meal. If he becomes impatient, stop and try again later. Carry out each stage gently and calmly, giving occasional treats to make the whole experience positive.

BRUSHES AND COMBS

Different types of brushes and combs are available, but they are not all suitable for every cat.

Soft-bristled brush: soft, plastic bristles have a smoothing action. Not suitable for detangling long hair.
Rubber-toothed brush or glove: soft, smoothing action. Good for massage but not suitable for detangling mats.
Metal-pinned brush: thin metal pins have a slight detangling action. Can be used on long and short hair but will not detangle heavy mats.
Metal-toothed comb: solid, metal pins have a stiff detangling action. Suitable for longhaired cats if used carefully but too harsh for very shorthaired varieties.

STEP BY STEP

1. Detangling

Use a metal-toothed comb to tease out any matting. Start at the end of the tangle furthest from the skin and work up. Remember that a mat may be tugging on your cat's skin so be very gentle.

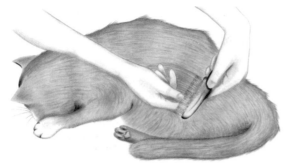

Always try to detangle knots first, but if you can't you will have to cut them away. Your cat's skin is very loose and can easily be snipped if you are not careful, so use a small pair of scissors. Cut away a small amount at a time and follow each cut by teasing out the hair until the mat comes away altogether. If the matting is widespread and you do not feel confident doing it yourself, contact a vet or professional groomer who will be able to help you.

2. Brushing the body

Once any mats are removed you can comb through the rest of the fur. Start on the back and move in the direction that the fur grows. Then move down the sides, legs and tail. If the fur is very long, take small sections at a time and comb each section carefully. Make small strokes rather than long sweeping ones, so that you don't accidentally snag your cat's fur.

3. Brushing the head

Head grooming is not essential for most cats, but yours may enjoy it. Use a small, soft-bristled brush and move in the direction the fur lies. Brush only the top of the head and the cheeks; do not try to brush near the eyes, nose or mouth.

4. Clipping the claws

Cats should have their front claws clipped as and when they need it – usually every three or four months. When the claws are fully extended the tip of your cat's claw should not reach beyond the base of his paw. A cat that spends a lot of time outside may not need his claws trimming quite as often as an indoor-only cat, although if you provide indoor scratching posts and climbing towers there may not be much difference.

Special cat claw clippers, available from pet shops and vets, are small, easy to use and safe; scissors could shatter the claw. Begin by stroking your cat's paw and then holding it for a second. Repeat this a few times, each time increasing the length of time you hold his paw. Once you can hold it for a few seconds, you can start to push out his claws. Do this by putting your forefinger on the pad of the foot and your thumb above and slightly behind the claw, then press gently to extend the claw. You may find this easier if you position yourself behind your cat and face in the same direction as him.

Once you are holding the claw out, look for a clear outer section and a darker inner section. You should avoid cutting near the inner section as this is the blood-filled quick. If you can't see it, just trim the very tip of the longest claws. Repeat for all claws on the front paws.

Back claws are tougher and tend to shatter when clipped, but they seldom need doing anyway because they are not sharpened like the front claws. Leave them unless you think it is absolutely necessary.

IF YOUR CAT WON'T LET YOU GROOM HIM

If your cat isn't used to being groomed regularly he may resist it or disappear at the sight of a brush. There is no quick solution and you certainly shouldn't restrain him or you will find he is unlikely ever to come around to the idea of being groomed.

The only answer is to use a soft brush and carry out very short grooming sessions that you increase over time. Keep the brush near to where you tend to settle down with your cat for the evening – this way you can groom him when he is really relaxed.

If he is scared of a particular brush, you should consider changing it for a different coloured brush that he won't recognize.

How to wash a cat

Few adult cats enjoy being bathed and you will only have to wash your cat if he gets something particularly bad in his fur or if your vet has recommended it as a treatment. Otherwise, unless you plan to show him, it is advisable to leave the washing to him.

If you decide that you want to wash your cat regularly anyway, it is best to start when he is a kitten.

Preparing
First you must completely brush your cat's fur so that there are no knots. Then you will need an apron, a plastic jug, a bath towel and a bottle of cat shampoo (do not use detergents or human shampoos). Finally, pour about 3 cm of lukewarm water into a bath or sink and then get your cat. It is a good idea to close the door behind you in case of any escapes.

Getting him wet
Place your cat in the water, reassuring him all the time. Hold him with one hand across his chest to steady him and then scoop up some water in the jug and gently pour it over his back. Repeat this until his body is completely wet. Do not try to wash his head or face.

Shampooing
Pour shampoo across his back and on to his sides, then lather it gently until you have done his back, belly, tail and legs.

Rinsing
Use the jug, or preferably a shower nozzle, to rinse the shampoo out with clean water. Keep rinsing until you are sure that all traces of shampoo are gone.

Drying
Finally, get the bath towel and wrap your cat up. Lift him out of the bath and place him down on the floor where you can gently massage most of the water out of his fur. Once you've finished, allow him to sit somewhere warm and cosy to finish off drying. Give him some treats but do not let him go outside until he is completely dry.

Alternatives to water
If you just need to give an old cat a helping hand or want to remove something unpleasant from your cat's fur, you do not have to place him in water. You can buy cat-safe wipes – similar to baby wipes – or simply get a clean, damp tea towel to wipe his fur down.

CLEANING EYES, NOSE AND EARS

Clean your cat's eyes and ears only as and when it is required. Some cats hardly ever need this done, but for others it may be part of a regular grooming regime. Very flat-faced or long-faced breeds, such as the Persian or Siamese, are prone to excess discharge around the eyes or nose; other longhaired breeds may also be unable to clean themselves properly and so will need extra help.

Clean the eyes and nose if there is a light discharge collecting near them. If the eyes look very sore and red, or if there is an excess of discharge that continues to be produced from either the eyes or nose, you should take your cat to the vet.

Some wax in the ears is normal, but if there is an excess of ear wax or if the ears smell slightly, then you should clean them. If the ears seem very smelly or if they appear to have dark, gritty matter inside them, you should take your cat to the vet because he may be suffering from ear mites.

Eyes and nose
Wet a cottonwool ball with clean water or an eye-cleaning solution and squeeze out the excess liquid. Press the cottonwool ball into the dirty area and pull away from the eye or nostril. Repeat using a clean part of the cottonwool ball for each stroke and using separate cottonwool balls for each eye and the nose.

Ears
Wet a cottonwool ball with water or a special ear-cleaning solution and squeeze out the excess liquid. Use the cottonwool ball to wipe inside the ear. Push the cottonwool ball into the outer part of the ear and twist. Be very careful not to push too hard as the ears are easily damaged.

CLEANING TEETH
It is a good idea to clean your cat's teeth regularly. For more information on this, see page 83.

SLEEP, PLAY AND EXERCISE

In the wild, cats spend much of their time sleeping to conserve energy for short, energetic bursts of hunting. Your cat's life should be very similar to this.

Sleep

There is nothing quite like a cat curled up beside you, snoring away, to make you feel peaceful. Sleep is what cats do best, and on average they do it for about 16 hours a day – that's twice as long as you. This sleep is the key ingredient for a long and healthy life, and your cat should be given plenty of safe, warm places to rest undisturbed.

You can purchase a range of different cat beds, from a hammock that hooks on to radiators to a simple blanket. Buying a bed is not essential, as cats tend to alternate their sleeping spots between various beds, sofas and floors around the house. However, a nervous cat may appreciate an 'igloo' bed that increases his sense of security.

An igloo bed helps this timid cat feel secure.

Play

Play releases pent-up energy, which reduces stress and burns calories. It also provides an outlet for natural behaviours such as hunting and scratching.

If your cat isn't given the opportunity to play, he could become overweight and lose body condition. He is also more likely to develop 'behaviour problems'. These are often just natural behaviours that are not being given sufficient outlet in his day-to-day activities and include things like ankle-ambushing – when your cat pounces on your feet as you walk past, which can result in your or his injury (see page 105).

Play is important for all cats, but it is essential for indoor-only cats who do not get the chance to hunt, climb and scratch outside in a natural way. These cats can easily become bored and may act out their frustration on you, your furniture or your walls. You can help prevent this by setting aside time each day to play with your cat and providing an environment rich in toys, climbers and scratching posts.

TWO CATS

Having two cats can be a great help because they can play with and amuse each other much of the time that you are not at home. But be warned: two cats mean twice the cost and twice the trouble, so do think carefully about whether you can deal with two sets of vet's bills, food bills, insurance premiums and all the other costs.

Playing with another cat is a great way to release pent-up energy, socialize and get some exercise.

PLAYING WITH YOUR CAT

From your cat's point of view, the best games are ones that involve you. Interactive games help to let off steam, form bonds between you and your cat, and more closely resemble the stalking, chasing and pouncing of natural hunting behaviour.

How often you play with your cat is up to you, but a couple of 5- to 10-minute bursts of activity a day should be fine for an adult indoor–outdoor cat. An indoor-only cat will need more regular play times and mental stimulation, and a kitten can play almost indefinitely.

It's all very well throwing down a toy mouse for your cat, but it provides only limited fun. The best games are ones where you pull or dangle something for him to chase. This keeps your hands out of the way while your cat can use his weaponry to full effect.

This overweight cat is being encouraged to play.

Working out how to get some dried food out of a glass jar is giving this cat mental stimulation and exercise.

Toys and Games

You won't be able to resist buying some of the huge number of toys available in supermarkets and pet shops, but you can also create alternatives for free, and it's a good idea to rotate toys from time to time anyway.

Chasing games

The best types of toys are called 'fishing rod' or 'teaser' toys. They involve a length of string or bendy cord with a toy or feather attached to the end. Your cat will love playing with one of these: not only does it involve you, but it is also more realistic to chase something that actively moves and changes direction and speed, so helping to exercise his hunting instinct.

Instead of buying one, you can always use an old soft belt (e.g. from a dressing gown), or a length of string – although do put string away after playing with it as kittens have been known to swallow it.

There are also a huge number of toy mice and balls available that your cat can bat around, though they do provide limited enjoyment because they don't move independently. Try toys filled with catnip to get an extra reaction from him, or simply crunch up a ball of foil for your cat to chase.

This cat is exercising and practising his hunting skill as he plays with this catnip-filled mouse.

Food-finding games

If your cat is a bit reluctant to play, or if you feel he needs more mental stimulation, try games that reward him for working things out.

You can buy toys that randomly release treats as your cat plays with them, but you can just as easily make your own. Take a clean plastic bottle and cut a few holes in it that are only just bigger than the treats that you are going to use. Put the treats inside, screw the top back on and place the bottle on the floor. You may have to tap it a few times so your cat gets the idea, but leave him to work out how to get the treats out. If your cat is overweight, use a portion of his daily dried food allowance instead of treats to help him shed some pounds while he's getting fed.

Alternatively, try putting a few pieces of dried food in a paper (not plastic) bag on a window sill or in a glass jar for your cat to seek out while you are out at work.

Choose Games Carefully

It is important to think about the games you teach a kitten – don't teach him games you don't want him to play later. It may feel harmless when a little kitten chases and grabs your fingers or toes, but it will feel much more serious when he's fully grown. It's best to use games that are one step removed from direct contact so he will not misinterpret your or anyone else's actions as a game.

Crazy about catnip

Catnip or catmint (*Nepeta cataria*) is a plant which secretes an oil that sends some cats into a state of crazy happiness. It affects about 40 per cent of cats (the others don't have the right gene) and is completely harmless; the effects wear off after a while, but if you put the toy away and bring it out later, your cat will go loopy all over again.

You can buy dried catnip loose to rub on toys and scratchers (see page 72), or you can buy toys and treats stuffed with catnip to give your cat that extra buzz.

71

Scratching and climbing

Most cats love to have a good scratch and a climb; doing these things lets off steam and stretches the muscles. One of the most important pieces of equipment for a happy cat is a scratching post because it allows him to carry out a very important natural behaviour and deters him from using your furniture. Climbing is a good way for your cat to exercise, though some cats do it more than others.

Cats Need to Scratch

Cats scratch to stretch their muscles, to keep their claws in good condition and to mark their scent on important parts of their territory. Have at least one scratching post and keep it in a prominent area of the house. If you keep your cat indoors all the time, he will probably need more scratching posts, so get a couple and add to them if necessary.

A scratching post should be tall enough to allow your cat to reach full stretch when using it; very steady so that it doesn't move or topple over; and made of hard-wearing material, such as wood covered in sisal. Scratching posts can be upright or angled – some cats will use both and others prefer one type: trial and error is the only way to find out.

This indoor–outdoor cat gets plenty of chances to scratch outside, but would still appreciate a scratching post.

Don't prevent scratching

Scratching only becomes a 'behaviour problem' if you have provided your cat with plenty of opportunity to use scratching posts but he still continues to use places that you think are inappropriate.

It is far better to look at why your cat is scratching inappropriately than to try to prevent him from doing it permanently because scratching helps a cat feel secure and happy. Two unhelpful 'solutions' are declawing – the permanent amputation of a cat's claws, which is banned in the UK – and plastic caps fitted over the cat's claws so

he can no longer scratch. Although plastic caps are a far better solution than declawing, both of these methods merely transfer the problem and can result in far worse habits. For more information on solutions to problem scratching, see page 104.

Climbing and Jumping

Being able to climb freely helps to keep your cat's body in tip-top condition and provides an outlet for energy. Some cats seldom jump or climb, while others are true explorers and can be found on curtain rails, on top of wardrobes or perched on doors.

Climbing and jumping can be carried out anywhere around your house, but you can also provide your cat with a climbing tree or activity tower. Cat towers come in all sorts of shapes and sizes but usually involve platforms suspended on climbing poles. The more complex and expensive towers have many different levels and include cosy beds, cubby holes, toys suspended on strings and scratching posts.

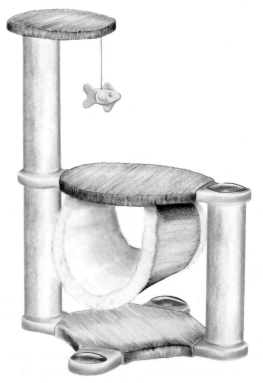

A climbing tree like this one combines a scratcher, toy and climbing frame in one.

MOVING YOUR CAT

Cats don't like to be moved out of their familiar territory, but there are occasions when it is unavoidable. Careful preparation can make the process as simple as possible for both you and your cat.

What you will need

CARRIERS

The most important piece of equipment you will need for transporting your cat is his carrier. These come in many shapes and sizes and can vary in quality, but the best carriers give your cat plenty of room to sit, lie down and turn around comfortably, have a solid tray base to help catch any 'little accidents' and open at the top for easy access.

Metal carriers are very robust so are often used by people who work in animal welfare.

If you will be making long journeys with your cat, space is of particular importance and you may want to choose a carrier that has integrated food and water bowls. If you plan to transport your cat by air, you will need to check that the carrier you plan to use is approved by the airline that you are flying with.

Hard carriers (£20–£60)

Wicker carriers are preferred by some owners because they are the most attractive to look at but they do not have a solid base to catch urine and they can be quite tricky to clean.

Metal carriers are the most hard-wearing and usually provide the widest opening for getting a cat in. They are often used by rescue organizations but they do not have a solid base to catch urine so can be unsuitable for transporting a cat in your own car.

Plastic carriers are by far the most suitable for general use because they normally have a solid base to catch urine, are easy to clean and they are hard-wearing enough for most cat owners' needs.

Soft carriers (£20–£40)

These carriers are usually made of a solid frame covered with hard-wearing canvas. They can often be disassembled so they lie flat, which is useful if you don't have much room for storage. They are not suitable if you are taking your cat on a long journey, particularly if he will be going by air.

Cardboard carriers (£3–£8)

A cardboard carrier should only be used for a brief single journey because it can easily become weak with repeated use and will be damaged if your cat urinates in it.

USEFUL EXTRAS

Newspaper

If your cat doesn't travel well he may urinate or vomit, so it is a good idea to line the base of your carrier with newspaper. Take some spare sheets with you as well.

Blanket or cloth

Over the top of the newspaper, put a blanket or soft piece of cloth to make the carrier comfortable. Take a spare one on longer journeys in case you need to change it.

FOOD AND DRINK

If you are going on a journey that is over three hours long, you should take some water for your cat. You may want to give him some dried food as well, but if he suffers from motion sickness and your journey is less than six hours long, it is best to refrain from feeding him until you have reached your destination.

This plastic carrier opens at the top to allow easy access and has a solid bottom so that accidents don't damage upholstery.

Preparation

Before you put your cat in a carrier and travel with him,
it pays to prepare for the journey.

GETTING USED TO THE CARRIER

Getting your cat used to his carrier is the first step in any journey, whether it is 15 minutes to the vet or six hours on a flight. Many cats don't like being confined in such a small space and the more familiar he is with his carrier the less trouble you are going to have when it comes to putting him in it.

Leave your cat carrier out and open so your cat can rub his scent on it and can walk in and out without being shut in. Do this for a minimum of three days prior to your journey, or for longer if you can.

If you can get your cat to use his carrier as a bed by putting one of his favourite blankets in it, then this would be ideal.

GETTING USED TO TRAVEL

If you want to prepare your cat as much as possible, you can take him out in his carrier for a few very short journeys first, perhaps just shutting the door while he is inside at first and then moving on to walking with him in the carrier and then taking him out for a few minutes in the car.

When you take on a young kitten, you will be responsible for how he views his carrier and travelling from the start, so taking it slowly will be of great benefit. If you have rehomed an older cat, the chances are that his reaction to travelling will already have been set, but it is always a good idea to take things slowly anyway so that you don't strengthen his fears.

BEFORE YOU GO

Give yourself plenty of time to prepare for your journey. Make sure that your cat is kept in the night before you travel and that he does not get outside the next day. No matter how hard we try to hide an impending trip in the carrier, cats just seem to have a sixth sense about these things and will often disappear if given half a chance.

If you do feed your cat on the day, give him only a very small meal and don't feed him anything for at least three hours before your journey, particularly if he is prone to motion sickness. Give him the opportunity to use a litter tray right up until you are ready to leave.

Prepare everything you need before you put your cat in his carrier so you can leave as soon as he is in. Don't leave him sitting around in the carrier for any longer than is necessary.

Getting a cat used to his carrier gradually over time will make for much easier journeys in the future.

PETS – the Pet Travel Scheme

PETS is a system of certification for animals being transported between EU (and a few non-EU) countries.

If you are bringing your cat into the UK from another qualifying country and he has a Pet Passport he can enter without having to undergo quarantine (see below).

You can apply for a Pet Passport through your vet. To qualify, your cat must be microchipped, vaccinated against rabies and must have a blood test, in that order. He will then have to wait for six months before being free to travel to prove he hadn't contracted rabies before the vaccination was given.

To keep your Pet Passport valid, your cat must have his rabies booster vaccinations on time. If he misses a deadline, he will have to be re-tested and wait a further six months before travelling again.

Any cat coming into the UK must be treated against ticks and tapeworms not less than 24 hours and not more than 48 hours before being checked in. This must be done by a vet using specific products. Your cat must then travel in an IATA-approved carrier that allows him to stand, sit, lie down and turn around naturally, with suitable ventilation and no spaces big enough for the cat to get any part of his body, such as his tail or paw, out of the carrier while it is secure. Your cat should travel with an IATA-approved carrier company and via an IATA-approved route.

Your cat will not be allowed to travel if he or she is ill or injured, too young, has recently given birth or is heavily pregnant. If your cat has to be sedated for travel, this can only be done under veterinary guidance and your cat must be accompanied by a certificate.

A Pet Passport can get your cat to and from many countries without the need for six months in quarantine.

The journey

BY CAR

Always put your cat somewhere secure and safe in the car so that he doesn't shift about. Some carriers can be strapped into a standard seatbelt – like the one shown at the bottom of page 73 – but others may need to be put into the foot well. Don't put your cat in the boot because not only is this area more susceptible to accidents but it can also take in fumes from the exhaust.

Drive carefully and smoothly and keep your cat in his carrier throughout the journey. If you need to change his newspaper or water, make sure that there is no possibility of escape while he is out of the carrier.

BY TRAIN

You are allowed to take up to two cats on a train without charge. They must be kept in a rigid carrier at all times and are not allowed to take up a seat space.

BY BUS

You can take your cat on the bus as long as he is kept in a rigid cat carrier at all times.

BY PLANE

Whether you are flying within the UK or on an international flight, it is always best to contact the airline to find out what their rules and regulations are, as they differ from one company to another. Taking your cat abroad may need a lot of preparation, often as much as six months.

Taking your cat abroad

Every country has different rules and schemes for the transportation of live animals, so you should carefully research the requirements of the country or countries that you are planning to take your cat to and always consult their embassies. If you take your cat out of your own country, you will not necessarily be able to bring him back in without restrictions.

Transporting your cat from one country to another is a relatively complicated process and, although it is quite possible to arrange transportation yourself, many people choose to hire an animal transportation company to help organize the trip for them.

QUARANTINE

In some cases, your cat may be coming from or going to a country that does not qualify for the PETS scheme (above). In these cases, he may have to remain in quarantine for six months before entering the country.

Quarantine is a period that animals have to spend in isolation to check that they have not contracted a contagious disease. This is usually six months spent in the destination country at an approved cattery.

This cat awaits his release after a six-month stay in quarantine.

Moving house

Moving house is not only stressful for us humans but is an incredibly big deal for your cat too. Much of his feeling of safety and security comes from the familiar sights, sounds and smells around him and altering these in such a dramatic way can be very upsetting. Careful planning will help moving day go smoothly for you and for him.

First you must decide what you are going to do with your cat on moving day. You can either book him into a cattery for a few days or move him with you.

CATTERY

The cattery option is often the best solution because it means that you can take your cat away from all the unfamiliar noise and movement and leave him in a place of peace and quiet while you deal with all the upheaval. Don't forget to book well in advance and make sure his vaccinations are up to date.

If you are moving close by, you can take your cat over to the cattery first thing on the morning you are moving. If you are moving across the country, it would be better to book a cattery near your new house so that when you collect him there will be only a short journey to his new home. (For more on catteries, see page 77.)

Once you have brought your cat home, the following advice on settling him in after the move should help make the transition easier.

Make sure you are completely ready to leave before you put your cat in his carrier.

MOVING WITH YOUR CAT

If you decide to keep your cat with you when you move, you need to plan ahead. The following guide should help.

One to two weeks before the move

Pick a 'safe' room in both your current and your new house where you can put your cat while all your belongings are moved. Both rooms need to be out of the way and easily closed off. Clear the 'safe' room in your current house of any furniture and put your cat's bed, scratching post, toys, cat carrier, litter tray, and food and water bowls in there. Start to feed him there to get him used to his room.

The night before

The evening before your move, put your cat in his room, making sure he cannot escape through any windows or other openings and close the door. If you are going to have removal people in your house, you may want to put a sign on the door warning them that your cat is in there and that he is not to be disturbed. Many calm and balanced cats will be quite relaxed about strange people coming into their house, but it is best not to risk your cat being scared off and disappearing just before you are due to hand the keys over to the new owners.

On the day

Keep your cat in his room, making sure that his litter tray is kept clean and that he is as undisturbed as possible. If you are not leaving until later in the afternoon, you can feed him a small meal first thing but don't give him any food for three or four hours before you leave.

Wait until you are ready to leave, then pack up all your cat's things in a bag and put him into his carrier to transport him to your new house.

Once you arrive, take him to his 'safe' room, close the door behind you and then unpack his things. Open his carrier but don't force him to come out – just make sure he has a litter tray, a bowl of water and some food and then leave the room. Make sure that you put a sign on the door to warn the removal people not to disturb him.

A few days later

Keep your cat in his safe room for a few days until he is feeling more confident. It can be overwhelming to have access to a whole new house straight away, so a little-by-little approach is always best. Make sure that when you let him out of his safe room all doors, windows and cat flaps to the outside world are closed.

Three to four weeks later

It is best to give your cat this amount of time to become accustomed to his new surroundings before letting him outside (see page 48 on how best to do this).

Many cats go missing just after they have been moved because they are let outside too soon; in these cases they are often found trying to make their way back to their old home. If your cat is microchipped, don't forget to change your address details on the register so that if he goes missing he can be returned to you.

LEAVING YOUR CAT

There are a number of ways that you can arrange for your cat to be cared for when you are away from home. The most popular choice is to put him into a cattery, but you can also employ petsitters, homesitters and friends or family. Which one you choose depends on how your cat reacts to different situations, what you can afford and what you feel most comfortable with.

Catteries

Catteries are the most popular choice for cat owners. In a cattery, the cats are kept in rows of enclosed pens. Usually there is some sort of outside run, but they can be indoor-only pens. Catteries vary quite considerably, so it is a good idea to go and have a look at a few before you decide. They cost around £8–£10 per day for a single cat.

If you plan to use a cattery, make sure it is registered by the local council as this will ensure that it meets a minimum set of care standards. If you want to be assured of the highest level of accommodation and care for your cat, look for either of the following:

- FAB-approved catteries – the Feline Advisory Bureau keeps a list of catteries that have been passed by a FAB inspector.
- KOBrA kite mark catteries – the Kennel Owners and Breeders Association also has a kite-mark scheme whereby catteries are examined and assessed by a KOBrA inspector.

WHAT TO LOOK FOR

- The cattery and buildings should look and smell clean and tidy.
- A local authority cattery licence should be displayed on the wall – if not, ask to see it.
- Cats should each have their own runs and sleeping compartment (unless the cats are from the same family).
- There should be a gap or solid wall (glass or Perspex) between each unit so that cats can't have any physical contact with their neighbours.
- To prevent escapes, there should be an anti-escape corridor between the pens and the outside world.
- Sleeping compartments should have some form of heating and be protected from wind, sun and rain.

The owner and staff

The people who run the cattery should be caring, knowledgeable and friendly and, before they take your booking, they should ask you certain questions, including:

- Has your cat been neutered?
- Does he have any health problems or need medication?
- Does your cat have any special dietary requirements?
- Are his vaccinations up to date?

BOOK EARLY AND BE PREPARED

As soon as you know you are going away, book your cattery. Good catteries get booked up very early, particularly during busy holiday times such as summer, Christmas and half-term holidays.

Before you go, make sure your cat's vaccinations are up to date because the cattery owner will ask to see his vaccination record and will not be able to take your cat without it. Ask someone you trust if you can leave their details with the cattery owner in case there is an emergency while you are away.

Alternative care

If you don't have a cattery near you that you want to use, there are some alternatives available.

PETSITTERS OR HOMESITTERS

A petsitter is someone who will come to your house each day to feed your cat and spend a short time with him. They will often carry out other tasks like watering your plants or feeding a goldfish. Depending on where you are based, they cost between £5 and £15 per visit.

A homesitter will actually stay in your house while you are away. They will provide constant company for your cat and extra security for your home but they are more expensive at about £30–£40 per day.

Many people find these types of services useful if their cat reacts badly to being in a cattery or if they have quite a few animals that all need caring for, but you must be careful to use a reputable company because you will be giving strangers access to your home. You can find details of pet- and homesitters near you by checking your local directories or contacting the National Association of Registered Petsitters (see page 126).

PET OWNERS' EXCHANGE

These are exchange systems where you and another pet owner in your area agree to look after each other's pets for free when you each go on holiday. You may find details of these locally or you can contact Pet Sitter Swap (see page 126).

FRIENDS AND FAMILY

The best of all worlds is if you have friends, neighbours or family nearby who can help you out by feeding your cat and spending some time with him while you are away.

IDENTIFICATION

You should always identify your cat in case he gets lost or stolen and needs to be returned to you. There are two main types of identification: microchips and collars. There are advantages and disadvantages to each, so many people use both. If you use only one, it should be a microchip.

Microchip

Microchips are a permanent, safe and tamper-proof form of identification but they can only be read with a scanner.

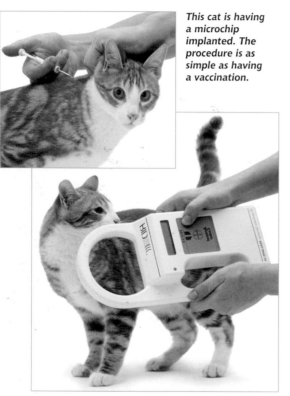

This cat is having a microchip implanted. The procedure is as simple as having a vaccination.

The implanted microchip is read with a scanner.

The microchip is a tiny device about the size of a grain of rice that is implanted under the skin in between your cat's shoulder blades. Any vet or qualified microchip implanter can perform the procedure, which takes just a moment. The microchip is coded with a unique number that is specific to your cat and lasts for his lifetime. The code is kept on a database with your contact information. Once a microchip is implanted, the unique code can be read by a scanner to retrieve the owner's contact details.

Collar and tag

Collars are an easily visible form of identification, but there are some safety issues associated with them and they can easily be lost or removed.

A collar is fitted round your cat's neck and has an engraved tag that includes information such as the cat's name and your contact telephone number. There are two main types of collars available – standard and safety.

Standard collars are very secure because they are buckled and have either no give or limited give in them. Unfortunately, there have been many incidents of cats getting entangled in branches or other objects, or getting their legs or jaws stuck in these types of collars, resulting in severe injuries or strangulation.

Safety collars are sometimes referred to as snap-release or quick-release collars. They are attached via a clip section that releases under pressure, such as when the cat gets caught on something. This type of collar is much safer than a standard collar, but because it can easily be lost or removed by a cat that doesn't want to wear it, it is always best to microchip your cat as well.

Fitting a collar

To fit a collar, make sure that you can get two fingers underneath it when it is on your cat. It should be snug so it cannot easily get caught on objects, but it must not restrict your cat's throat.

If you use a collar on a kitten, you should regularly check to make sure that it still fits properly, as kittens can grow out of their collars quickly. You should also check an adult cat's collar from time to time to ensure that it still fits well.

Your cat's collar fits properly if you can place two fingers in between the collar and your cat's neck.

LOSING YOUR CAT

How to find him

If your cat has gone missing there are many steps you can take to give yourself the best chance of finding him again.

1. Check your house

It may sound silly, but on many occasions cats that go missing are found in their own houses. Cats have a habit of getting into everything and all it takes is someone to come along and close a door and the cat is trapped. Check in cupboards, washing machines, up chimneys and in any awkward spaces. Even if you think it is impossible for a cat to become stuck somewhere, look anyway because you would be surprised where they can end up.

2. Inform the microchip register

If he is microchipped, you should ring your microchip provider to inform them that your cat is missing.

3. Check the surrounding area

Check your own garage, shed and greenhouse, as well as having a good look round your garden.

LOST CAT

Jessie

Tortoiseshell cat with a white chest and paws. Wearing a red collar and tag when she went missing but is also microchipped. Last seen on 27 September.

Please phone 05430 543 027.

4. Tell your neighbours

Inform all your neighbours. If your IT skills allow, it is best to print off some A4 or A5 posters with a clear photograph of your cat, a description (including any distinguishing marks) and your telephone number. Leave these with your neighbours and ask if they would mind checking their own garages and sheds.

5. Contact police, vets and animal charities

Give your local police, vets and animal rescue centres a description of your cat and your contact details. Ask your local vets and animal charities if you can send or drop off a poster for them to put up on their noticeboards.

6. Put up posters

Put posters up in local shops and use community newsletters and local newspapers to appeal for your cat.

If you have recently moved, follow the same steps in your old area as well, because your cat may have made his way back 'home'.

Chapter 4

YOUR CAT'S HEALTH

Provide your cat with a happy, safe environment and a balanced diet and he should live a largely problem-free life. However, just like you, your cat can suffer from illness, infection or injury and, when he does, you must be ready to help him recover.

Prevention is always better than cure. The first rule of cat care is to take regular action against the common preventable health problems that your cat may suffer. You will save yourself a lot of time and hassle in the long run, as well as saving your cat much discomfort and misery.

However, many illnesses are impossible to prevent and difficult to predict, although some are more likely to affect very young or old cats. The second rule, then, is to familiarize yourself with the more common ailments so that you can be aware of the symptoms and spot them early on.

PREVENTATIVE CARE

Many health problems are entirely preventable with a
little bit of forethought. Carrying out proper preventative
care for your cat can reduce your vet bills considerably.

Neutering

One of the most important things to do for your cat, and for
the cat population as a whole, is to neuter him or her.

There are around 2.5 million stray cats in the UK and
animal charities are overflowing with thousands of
unwanted cats and kittens, many of whom never find new
homes. The only way to reduce these numbers is to stop
more unwanted kittens being born. Cats are sexually active
from just four months old and are quite happy to mate
with siblings or other family members. If that doesn't
persuade you, then also remember that neutering has
many health benefits and will make your cat much easier
to live with.

*Neutering your cat will avoid many unpleasant behaviours,
including aggression.*

THE FACTS ABOUT YOUR UN-NEUTERED MALE CAT

- He will go roaming away from home in search of a
  mate – sometimes for days – which increases his risk
  of being run over or lost.
- He will be more territorial and is likely to fight with
  other cats, increasing his chance of being injured or
  catching a serious disease such as feline
  immunodeficiency virus (FIV) or feline leukaemia virus
  (FeLV), which can be costly to treat and are eventually
  fatal (see page 88).
- He is more likely to scratch, spray urine indoors and
  be aggressive.
- He can develop tumours in his testicles.
- He can make an unlimited number of female cats
  pregnant. Even if you don't have female cats yourself,
  there are plenty of un-neutered and unwanted strays
  that could be made pregnant by your cat.

THE FACTS ABOUT YOUR UN-NEUTERED FEMALE CAT

- She can be responsible for over 20,000 descendants
  in just five years – remember, it's not just the kittens
  she produces but all the kittens that her kittens
  produce and so on.
- The idea that it is unfair or unnatural not to allow a
  cat at least one litter before she is neutered is a myth.
  Being pregnant and giving birth are not easy for a cat
  and provide no benefit for the mother at all.
- She can have up to three litters a year, with up to
  eight kittens in each litter. Having so many kittens is
  very demanding and can make your cat ill.
- She will become pregnant if allowed outside. Even if
  kept indoors, she will attract tom cats by wailing
  loudly and there is always the chance that she may
  escape or that a tom may get in.
- She is more likely to get injured or catch a serious
  disease such as FIV or FeLV (see page 88) through
  bites when mating.
- She can develop cancer of the uterus or ovaries and is
  more likely to develop mammary cancer if not
  neutered before the age of six months.

THE OPERATION

Neutering involves a simple operation to remove your
cat's sexual organs so that he or she cannot reproduce.
Female cats, known as queens, are spayed (have their
ovaries and uterus removed). Male cats, known as toms,
are castrated (have their testes removed).

Cats can be neutered from four months old but you
should follow the advice of your vet.

You can usually drop your cat off and pick him or her
up on the same day. You will be asked to refrain from
feeding your cat prior to the operation – this is
something your vet will arrange with you beforehand.

After the operation, your female cat will have a small
shaved area on her side and some stitches. These may be
dissolvable; if not, they will need to be removed by the
vet after about ten days. She may be a bit quiet at first
but should recover within a week.

Male cats do not need stitches and will recover within
a few days.

Cost

The cost of the operation varies depending on where
you live, but is usually between £30 and £50 for a male
and between £40 and £70 for a female. Some charities
run schemes to help pay for neutering operations;
contact details are on page 126.

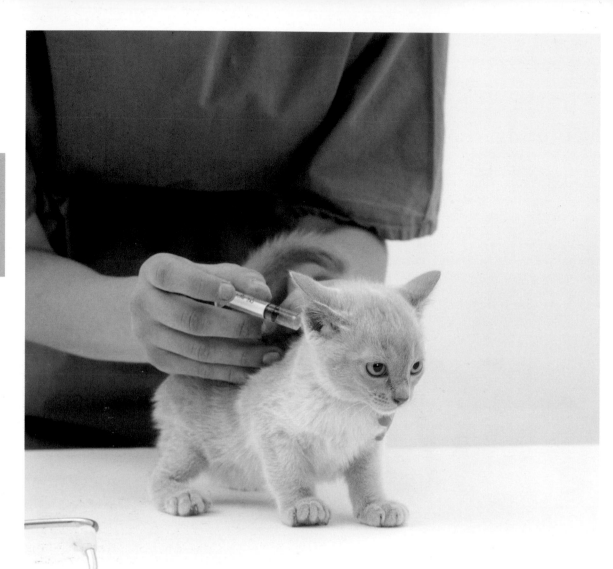

This nine-week-old kitten is having his first vaccination.

Vaccinations

Just like you, your cat can pick up diseases from his environment or from other cats. Vaccinations train your cat's antibodies to fight particular diseases to which he may be exposed and, as some of these diseases can be fatal, it is vital that you keep his vaccinations up to date.

There are many different vaccines available; some are essential but others will be recommended by your vet only if there is a high risk of exposure to a certain disease, such as if you are taking your cat abroad.

The three core vaccines used in the UK are for cat flu, feline parvovirus (FPV) (also know as feline infectious enteritis or feline panleucopenia) and feline leukaemia virus (FeLV) – see page 88 for more information on these diseases. Usually your vet will vaccinate against these three diseases in one single injection. Note, however, that some vets do not necessarily vaccinate against FeLV, so you should double check if you aren't sure.

WHEN TO VACCINATE

Kittens are usually vaccinated at about eight weeks old and then again at around twelve weeks. Your cat will then need one booster vaccination every year for the rest of his life. Whilst vaccines provide a very high level of protection, they can be less effective if given to a cat that is unwell, so always ensure your cat is healthy when he receives his vaccinations.

Cost

A single vaccine to protect against the three core diseases in the UK costs between £35 and £50, depending on the vet you use.

Dental care

It is very common for cats to suffer from tooth and gum problems, even from as young as three. Plaque builds up on their teeth forming tartar, which can cause tooth decay, tooth loss, gingivitis and stomatitis (see page 89). A regular teeth-cleaning routine will help keep your cat's teeth free from tartar and will prevent him suffering from serious gum disease.

Gingivitis and stomatitis are notoriously difficult to treat because there is no cure and, if they are severe, these conditions can leave your cat in considerable pain which may stop him eating.

This kitten is too young to have his teeth brushed properly, but very gentle introductions to the brush will mean he accepts brushing later.

Yellow plaque has clearly formed on this cat's teeth. Without a dental routine, he could develop a more serious problem.

A GOOD DENTAL ROUTINE

The best form of dental care is to brush your cat's teeth at least once a week to remove any build-up of plaque. This becomes an easy part of your routine if your cat is used to having his mouth handled and teeth touched from an early age. In reality, many owners neglect their cat's teeth until a problem is noticed and they are forced to brush them. Unfortunately, it can be difficult to convince an older cat to remain calm when having his teeth brushed if he has never experienced it before.

For a brush you can use a baby's toothbrush, a special cat toothbrush, a rubber fingertip brush or a small section of gauze wrapped around your finger – it will be trial and error to see which one your cat tolerates best. Use special cat toothpaste, not human toothpaste which can make your cat ill if he swallows it. Special cat tooth-brushing equipment is available from your vet or pet shop.

When to start

With cats under a year old, you can go through the motions of brushing teeth, using a soft brush with no toothpaste and very gently touching the teeth to get your cat used to the feeling of having his head held and teeth touched. After all his adult teeth have grown through (after his first year) you can begin brushing properly.

Difficulties

If your cat is very reluctant, start by putting a little toothpaste on your finger and making a circular motion across his teeth for only a few seconds. Gradually build this up over a few days, each time giving a treat after you have finished. When you move on to using a toothbrush, just clean one tooth at first and build this up over time.

There is no real substitute for brushing your cat's teeth, but if he will not tolerate brushing at all, ask your vet about these other available options:

Plaque control granules – powder that is sprinkled on to your cat's food to help reduce plaque build-up.
Dental food and treats – special dental foods and treats will help to control plaque, but they are not enough on their own to keep your cat's teeth healthy.

How to brush a cat's teeth

Wash your hands before you start and pull back your cat's lips to expose the teeth and gums. You will need to be careful but firm or your cat will wriggle away. Use your brush to make small circular motions across the front of the teeth. Do not brush behind the teeth. When you have finished, give your cat a nice treat so he associates the event with something pleasant.

Parasites

Parasites are creatures that live and feed off other living beings. The most common cat parasites are **fleas** and **worms**, which must be controlled with regular preventative treatment.

FLEAS

Fleas are very small creatures that survive by feeding on your cat's blood. They can reproduce at a very fast rate (each female flea can produce as many as 50 new eggs each day). These eggs will fall off your cat and hatch into larvae that can lie in wait in floorboards or carpets for up to two years before springing into action when they sense a suitable host nearby.

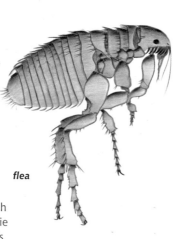

flea

Fleas may seem harmless, but they transfer infections and tapeworm (see page 85), can cause severe blood-loss in kittens and can bite you too (see page 96). Cats suffering from a serious flea infestation may scratch themselves so much that they cause open wounds, skin infections and hair loss.

Preventing fleas

It is best to prevent fleas rather than try to fight them once they have become established. There are many flea products available, including spot-ons, tablets, collars, sprays, foams and shampoos. The most popular and the easiest to apply are spot-ons, which are applied with a pipette directly to the skin on the back of the neck, usually once a month.

Flea treatments can be bought in pet shops and supermarkets, but the most effective are available only from your vet. The best treatments often have a multi-action and treat other less common parasites such as mites, lice or ticks at the same time. The different preparations vary in cost, but most are around £50 for 12 months' supply. You must be regular with your treatment and must treat all animals in the house.

Use the right treatment

Never use dog flea treatments on a cat because they can contain a substance called permethrin that is extremely toxic to cats. It is the biggest cause of poisoning in cats in the UK, with around 300 cases of serious poisoning every year and 30 fatalities.

This cat is having a spot-on flea treatment applied to the back of his neck.

Is it fleas?

It can be hard to spot fleas because they are very small and they move quickly, but if your cat is scratching more than usual he may have them.

If you suspect he has fleas, put him on a white sheet of paper and give him a good grooming with a fine-toothed comb. If he does have them, flea dirt (little black specks of dried blood) will be visible on the white paper. To test further, you can wet a cottonwool ball and dab it on to the black specks. If it is flea dirt it will gradually dissolve and become small streaks of blood.

If your cat is allergic to flea bites or is infested with fleas, his reaction will be much more severe. He may show hair loss where he has been scratching and have red or scabby skin, particularly around his neck and at the base of his tail.

Treating an outbreak

If your cat has suffered from an outbreak of fleas, you will need to prevent him being re-infested by larvae that have been shed in your house. To do this, use a flea control specifically made for houses. This usually involves spraying each room and leaving the spray to settle for a period of time before you or your cat can enter again.

Never use this same product directly on your cat. Instead continue to treat him regularly with a proper flea product made for cats.

WORMS

Worms rarely harm a cat but, if untreated, they can eventually obstruct the intestines and cause weight loss, vomiting and diarrhoea.

Cats are susceptible to two types of worms that can live in their gut or intestines:

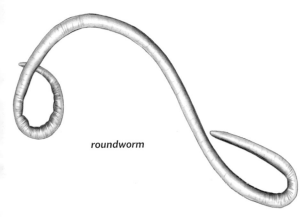

roundworm

Roundworms are very common. They resemble a cream-coloured earthworm but can grow to around 10 cm in length. They live in the intestine and feed on digested food. They release eggs into the cat's faeces which become infectious within a few days and remain so for many years. The eggs can also be passed through milk from a mother cat to her kittens.

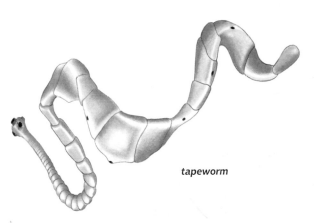

tapeworm

Tapeworms can infect most mammals and, as their name suggests, resemble a flat tape made of segments. Once inside the cat, they live by attaching themselves to the intestine and absorbing food. Segments from the tapeworm (which look like grains of rice) break off and are released in the cat's faeces. The segments then release eggs which infect other creatures like fleas or rodents. A cat only picks up the tapeworm when he eats an infected creature – he cannot become infected directly.

Both roundworms and tapeworms can infect humans, although this rarely happens (see page 97).

Preventing worms

There are many treatments for roundworm and tapeworm, some of which are effective against both and some of which are effective only against one or the other.

Tablets are the cheapest and most common form of treatment, but if you find it very difficult to give your cat tablets, other types, such as spot-ons, injections and pastes, are available. Treatments are available from supermarkets and pet shops but, as with flea products, the most effective treatments are available only from a vet.

Young kittens often suffer from roundworm rather than tapeworm, so they should be treated every two weeks from 6 to 16 weeks with a formula for roundworm. After 16 weeks, they should be treated for both roundworm and tapeworm. How often depends on the cat in question, but it is usually around every two to six months.

To stop re-infection with either roundworm or tapeworm, you should clean out faeces from your cat's litter tray as often as possible and regularly treat for fleas (see page 84) to stop cats (and potentially humans) being infected with tapeworm after swallowing an infected flea.

Is it worms?

A mild worm infection is hard to spot, but regularly treating your cat for both roundworm and tapeworm should keep them at bay. If your cat stops eating, is suffering from diarrhoea or is vomiting, then he may have a severe case of worms that is blocking his intestines.

You can check for tapeworm by looking for the released segments that resemble grains of rice. They may be found in bedding, in faeces or around the anus, and they may move.

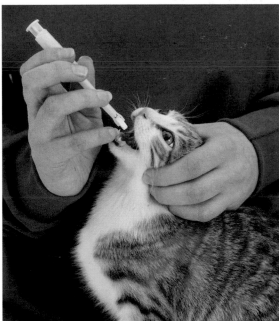

Some people find it easier to give their cat a tablet using a tablet applicator.

HEALTH A–Z

The following A–Z describes common conditions and signs of illness. It is a good idea to familiarize yourself with them so that you are able to recognize any signs of ill health at an early stage. If you are ever in doubt about your cat's health always contact your vet for advice. Never attempt to treat him using human medicine, even in small quantities, as this is more likely to harm than help him.

Cats are less likely to become ill if they are kept happy and healthy in the first place. Stress, overcrowding, poor diet, poor preventative healthcare and a lack of exercise can all contribute to an unhealthy cat. To find out more about what makes a cat happy, see Chapter 3.

Cross references to other entries in the A–Z appear in *italics*.

Appetite changes

A noticeable change in appetite – particularly a sudden one – can be a sign of many different illnesses and should be investigated by a vet.

Arthritis

A painful condition that affects the bone joints. Arthritis can occur gradually as an effect of old age or can be caused by injury to the bones. Symptoms, such as stiffness and lameness, tend to get worse over time and are often mistaken for old age. Arthritis cannot be cured, but pain and stiffness can be eased with medication, weight-loss regimes (for overweight cats) and occasionally surgery.

Asthma

Asthma is a collection of conditions that narrow the airways and constrict the lungs, causing breathing difficulties and coughing. You cannot prevent feline asthma, but medical treatment for long-term control of the disease is possible and avoiding triggers such as smoke, sprays or dust can reduce your cat's discomfort. Severe asthma attacks can be fatal.

Bad breath

Check your cat's teeth for sore gums and tartar build-up. Ensure you are brushing his teeth to keep them healthy (see page 83). Bad breath can be a sign of *gingivitis and stomatitis*.

Bleeding and wounds

Small scratches and grazes that aren't bleeding can be cleaned and left to heal. If a wound bleeds for more than a few seconds, is deep and longer than half a centimetre, or becomes infected, you should take your cat to the vet. Wounds caused by bites from other animals need to be seen by a vet quickly because high levels of bacteria in the mouth mean that abscesses may develop and a course of antibiotics is often needed. Check all wounds, even minor ones, periodically to make sure there is no sign of infection such as swelling, pain or pus at the wound site. As an infection becomes worse, it may be accompanied by an abscess, listlessness or reluctance to eat.

Cleaning a minor wound

Use cotton wool dipped in clean water or a salt solution – one teaspoon of salt dissolved in half a litre of cooled boiled water – to clean any dirt gently away. Pat the wound dry with a clean cloth and spread a thin layer of antiseptic cream over the affected area. Cat-safe antiseptic creams are available over the internet or from your vet. Savlon can be used as an alternative but many other human antiseptic creams, such as Germolene, contain substances that are toxic to cats.

Blindness

Blindness can have many causes and can involve either a partial or a complete loss of sight. Some conditions – such as glaucoma and cataracts – can be resolved with medication or surgery, but there are no guarantees that the problem will not return. Other conditions – such as progressive retinal atrophy or tumours – usually lead to irreversible blindness. Whether a cat can be treated or not depends on the nature and severity of the condition that is causing the blindness. Signs of blindness or eye disease include bumping into things (particularly recently moved furniture), confusion, discharge from the eye and changes in the appearance of the eye/s (e.g. one or both become swollen, cloudy or permanently dilated).

Blind cats should be kept indoors because it is difficult for them to sense dangers such as cars but, otherwise, cats adjust very well to the loss of sight in one or both eyes. As long as you provide an enriching environment, there is no reason why a blind cat should not live a full and active life. You should encourage your cat to find his own way about the house, try not to move furniture (as this will confuse him) and always talk to him as you approach him so that you don't startle him.

Breathing problems

Certain diseases, such as wet *FIP* and *asthma*, may cause breathing problems that recur, but other one-off problems can also cause breathing difficulties, including injury to the chest, insect *stings* near the face or throat, an obstruction in the airways or *poisoning*. Consult a vet immediately if your cat is having difficulty breathing or is panting with foam at the mouth. If your cat is panting with no other signs of stress, wait to see if 15 minutes' rest in a cool room resolves the problem before going to the vet.

Burns

Consult a vet if you notice burns on your cat. If you witness him getting burned and you can restrain him, you should hold the burn under cold water for 10 minutes before taking him to the vet. If you have to cover the burn it is best to use clingfilm rather than a piece of material, as this may have fibres that stick to the wound.

Cat flu

Cat flu is a common disease that can cause *sneezing*, dribbling, *coughing*, loss of appetite and a runny nose and eyes. It can be caused by a number of viruses and bacteria and is more likely to affect young cats, old cats or cats with weak immune systems. The disease is spread through direct contact between cats or contact via a third party such as people, clothing, food bowls and grooming equipment. It can sometimes be passed through sneezing.

There are no easy cures for cat flu and severe cases may be fatal. Although many cats do survive the disease they may go on to suffer recurring problems throughout life, such as intermittent bouts of flu-like symptoms, particularly a runny nose and sneezing. In some cases, cat flu can cause conjunctivitis (inflammation of the membrane surrounding the eye), which, without medical treatment, may lead to severe infection, *blindness* and ultimately the need to remove the affected eye/s. Cats can become carriers of the disease, sometimes for

This kitten's sore, red and weeping eyes suggest he may have cat flu.

several years after the original infection, so the condition is easily transferred from one cat to another.

Vaccines are available against most strains of cat flu and are included in your cat's yearly booster, which must be kept up to date to prevent infection – see page 82 for more details.

Convulsions or fitting

Convulsions are caused by abnormal brain functions and can be a result of epilepsy, *poisoning*, low blood sugar (*diabetes*), tumours, *injuries* or other disease. They are very frightening to experience but are rarely fatal. Your cat may show signs of disorientation and agitation, such as staggering, shivering, weakness or miaowing, both before and after a fit, but it is unlikely that you will be able to detect a fit before it happens unless your cat suffers from them regularly. Whilst the fit is taking place, avoid touching your cat unless he is in immediate danger, but do move any dangerous objects away from him. A fit may last a few seconds or a few minutes.

If your cat recovers from the fit quickly, consult your vet for advice, but if it lasts for more than five minutes, if your cat has another fit within half an hour, or if there are other signs accompanying the fit (e.g. foaming at the mouth or obvious wounds), you should take him to a vet as soon as possible.

Coughing

If your cat is coughing intermittently and retching he may simply have a hairball. If the coughing is accompanied by wheezing and a runny nose you should consult your vet.

Deafness

Deafness involves either partial or total loss of hearing. The causes of deafness fall into one of two categories. There is deafness caused by a blockage in the ear – mites, infection, wax build-up or tumours – which is often treatable with cleaning, antibiotics or surgery. Deafness can also be caused by

nerve damage – inherited and age-related conditions, deep infections, noise damage or damage caused by certain drugs – which is often permanent. If your cat doesn't respond when spoken to, is easily startled, miaows more loudly, seems dizzy, shakes his head, scratches his ears a lot or has some kind of discharge or pus coming from his ears, then he may be deaf or suffering from an ear infection. You should visit the vet to get a proper diagnosis and any possible treatment options. If your cat is permanently deaf it is better to keep him indoors out of the way of hazards; he will adapt very easily and will live an otherwise normal, happy life.

Dementia

Just like an elderly person, an elderly cat can suffer from dementia. This can take many forms, but often results in confusion, memory loss, a reduction in appetite and behavioural changes. For example, your cat may soil in the house because he forgets where the litter tray is, he may become irritable and afraid because he doesn't recognize you or other pets, and he may wake in the night and cry loudly because he doesn't know where he is. Some medications are available, but treatment may also involve a special diet, a specific exercise and play routine and an effort to keep the dementia sufferer's surroundings as stable as possible (e.g. not moving objects or furniture that may confuse your cat even more). Visit your vet to get a diagnosis before assuming dementia, as the signs are similar to many other health-related problems.

Diabetes mellitus

Diabetes mellitus is a disease that affects ability to control the blood-sugar level; signs include increased *thirst*, increased appetite, increased urination, weight loss, weakness and *vomiting*. It is more common in middle-aged and older cats, particularly if they are overweight. Treatment is more successful if started early and may involve insulin injections once or twice a day or oral medication. A diet may be prescribed to control blood sugar and to help an overweight cat lose weight (weight loss may cure the disease in some cases). Providing the right treatment is given, a diabetic cat will lead a relatively normal life for years to come.

Many people worry about coping with a diabetic cat, but advice is available from other diabetic cat owners via Cats Protection's Diabetic Register (see the contact section, page 126, for more details).

Diarrhoea

Mild diarrhoea that occurs for a period of 12–24 hours may be the result of a change in food or caused by your cat having eaten something unsavoury. If diarrhoea is severe or continues for more than 24 hours, consult a vet.

Dribbling

Dribbling may be a sign of teeth and gum problems, so you should talk to your vet if it is constant or is accompanied by a loss of appetite or pain. If your cat is also disorientated, foaming at the mouth or *convulsing*, consult a vet immediately.

Ear mites

Ear mites are tiny, spider-like creatures that live deep inside the ear and cause severe irritation to the ear canal. If left untreated, ear mites can cause swelling and infection. If your cat has ear mites, a dark wax will be visible inside his ear, and he may shake or scratch his head. Your

The waxy build-up and black specks seen in this cat's ear suggest he has ear mites.

vet can prescribe ear drops that you may need to apply for several weeks. With proper treatment your cat should suffer no permanent damage. Some flea treatments also offer protection against ear mites. Ask your vet for advice about whether one of these would be suitable for your cat.

Ear problems

If the ear swells up and seems painful, is bleeding a lot or has a discharge, visit your vet immediately. Mild to moderate scratching of the ears with no other problems may be a sign of fleas (see page 84) or ear mites.

Eye problems

A visible third eyelid (see page 38) is a general sign of an ill cat. If it is accompanied by other signs, then consult a vet, otherwise you should just watch for any developments.

Swelling, thick yellow or bloody discharge, changes in colour or obvious eye pain should be seen by a vet immediately. A light, watery, intermittent discharge can be bathed carefully with a cottonwool ball dipped in a saline solution. If the problem continues, consult your vet.

Feline Coronavirus
(FCoV) and Feline Infectious Peritonitis (FIP)

FCoV is a common and contagious virus that is passed through the faeces of cats. It does not affect humans or other animals, and rarely causes any problems in cats themselves – in most instances you will not even know your cat has the disease. However, in a very small percentage of cases, FCoV mutates into a fatal disease called FIP. There are two different types of FIP. Wet FIP causes a fluid build-up that makes the stomach swell and makes breathing difficult. Dry FIP can cause a loss of appetite, jaundice, a high temperature, and vision, behaviour or nervous system problems.

Sadly, there is no cure for FIP and most affected cats have to be euthanased (see page 94). There is no

vaccine but, although no one knows exactly what causes the disease to mutate, it is thought that minimizing stress, avoiding overcrowding and keeping litter trays and food areas separate and clean may help reduce the chance of FIP developing.

Feline Immunodeficiency Virus (FIV)

FIV is a virus that weakens the immune system, causing vulnerability to infections. It is similar to the human immunodeficiency virus (HIV) but it cannot be caught by humans. The virus is present in the blood, saliva and other body fluids. It is transmitted from cat to cat primarily through wounds inflicted through fighting and mating. There is no cure for FIV, but cats with the virus may show no signs for many years and so often lead otherwise normal lives. When symptoms do develop they include repeated bouts of illness, slow recovery from infections, weight loss and tumours. FIV-positive cats should be kept indoors to prevent the spread of the disease, and to protect the cat from other infections. They should be fully vaccinated and treated for fleas and worms to minimize the possibility of contracting a secondary disease. There is no vaccine for FIV. Getting your cat neutered (see page 81) is the best defence as it will reduce the risk of injuries gained through fighting and mating which help to spread the disease.

Feline Leukaemia Virus (FeLV)

FeLV is a virus that destroys the immune system, causing vulnerability to illness, including cancer. It is primarily transferred through the saliva or other secretions from the nose and mouth. It is most often spread by cats that live in close contact with each other through mutual grooming. The disease can also be passed in a mother's milk to her kittens, or from cat to cat in bites that occur when fighting or mating. It is more likely to affect young or weak cats and it does not affect humans.

Signs may not appear for months or years, but when they do develop they include repeated bouts of illness – such as infections, enlarged lymph nodes, anaemia and tumours with slow recovery times. FeLV-positive cats should be kept indoors to prevent spreading the disease and to protect the cat from other infections. They should also be fully vaccinated and treated for fleas and worms (see pages 84 and 85) to avoid the chance of catching a secondary disease. Sadly, around 80 per cent of cats diagnosed with FeLV die within three and a half years; many are euthanased because they have such a poor quality of life (see page 94).

To protect your cat against FeLV, you must keep his vaccinations up to date. The vaccination has no benefit if given after a cat has already contracted the disease – see page 82 for more details.

A poor coat condition like this can be a sign of illness.

Feline Lower Urinary Tract Disease (FLUTD)

FLUTD is a term used for a collection of conditions (including cystitis and urinary stones) that affect the urinary tract (bladder and urethra). FLUTD can be brought on by cancer, infection, muscle spasm, obstruction, stress or irritation of the bladder lining, but in the majority of cases no specific cause is found. Signs include pain or difficulty when urinating, an inability to pass urine, passing urine more frequently and only in small amounts, urinating in inappropriate places, blood in urine, behaviour changes and aggression. It is more common in old, overweight or indoor cats, and those that use a litter tray or eat an entirely dry diet. In male cats, it can be caused by an obstruction in the urinary tract; this is a life-threatening condition that requires immediate emergency surgery.

Cats with FLUTD usually need some form of long-term help because in most cases there is no cure. When managed properly, cats with FLUTD lead a relatively normal life. There is little you can do to prevent FLUTD, but a balanced diet that includes enough water, good

exercise and a stress-free environment will reduce the chance of your cat developing it.

Feline Parvovirus (FPV)

FPV is a serious disease and is also known as Feline Infectious Enteritis or Feline Panleucopenia. It particularly affects cats kept in multi-cat homes and is usually caught through infected faeces. Signs can include *vomiting*, a high or low temperature, hunger and *thirst* combined with an inability to eat or drink (the cat may sit bent over his bowl) and watery diarrhoea, sometimes with blood. Some cats die without any warning at all. Kittens that contract FPV through their mother can develop brain damage which makes their heads bob up and down and makes them unsteady on their feet.

There is no cure for FPV, but with early detection and intensive care many cats recover. Cats can be protected against FPV with their yearly booster vaccinations as long as they are kept up to date – see page 82 for more details.

Fleas

See page 84.

Fur problems

A poor coat condition (e.g. dull, dry, greasy or badly groomed) is a general sign of illness or can be the result of an inadequate diet. If a poor coat condition is accompanied by scabs or baldness, consult your vet. Mildly matted fur can be cut away carefully (see pages 67–68) but severe matting will need to be removed by your vet under anaesthetic.

Gingivitis and stomatitis

Gingivitis is an inflammation of the gums and stomatitis is an inflammation of the mouth. Both can cause bad breath, sore and bleeding gums, dribbling, ulcers,

Sore, red gums like these are a sign of gingivitis.

89

lack of appetite and a poor coat condition (grooming is neglected because the mouth is too sore). Mild cases of both are very common, particularly in kittens, but occasionally cats suffer from a severe inflammation that does not respond to treatment.

Cats with these conditions often require regular treatment, including special mouthwashes, diets and long-term medication. They may also need dental work, including the removal of some or all of their teeth. Surprisingly, cats cope very well without any teeth. Some cats will eventually recover, but others will require life-long help. Although it is not known what causes gingivitis and stomatitis, a good dental routine (see page 83) will help to keep your cat's teeth and gums healthy.

Heart murmur

A heart murmur (abnormal sounds coming from the heart) is often detected only by a vet listening to your cat's chest with a stethoscope. It can be caused by a heart defect that the cat is born with or that develops because of disease, or by other factors such as *high blood pressure*. The murmur may or may not affect how well the heart works. If it does, your cat may be tired, may breathe strangely, have pale gums or lose his appetite. A cat with a heart murmur may need medication or surgery but in many cases no treatment is needed, although your cat should still be checked regularly by a vet. Many cats with heart murmurs go on to lead normal lives, but if there is an underlying disease causing the murmur – such as heart disease – then the cat's health is likely to deteriorate over time and he may eventually need to be euthanased (see page 94).

High blood pressure

High blood pressure can occur as a result of another disease or it can be a problem in itself and can give rise to other conditions such as *heart murmur*, *diabetes*,

hyperthyroidism or kidney disease. It is sometimes known as hypertension. Signs may be few and far between at first, but they can include disorientation, seizures and changes in the eye (including *blindness* or bleeding). Depending on what causes the condition, your cat can go on to lead a relatively normal life.

Hypertension

See *High blood pressure*.

Hyperthyroidism

Hyperthyroidism is a condition where the thyroid gland produces too much of the hormone thyroxine. It is more common in middle-aged or older cats. Signs include an increased appetite, increased *thirst*, weight loss, restlessness, *vomiting*, *diarrhoea*, poor coat condition and an enlargement of the thyroid gland (at the base of the front of the neck). There are many different types of treatment, including medication, surgery to remove part or all of the thyroid gland and radiation treatment. Your cat may need medication for the rest of his life but, if the condition is detected and treated early on, he can go on to live an otherwise normal life.

If your cat constantly itches he may be suffering from skin parasites or other problems.

Injuries

Cats seldom hurt themselves but they can be involved in road traffic accidents and can get injuries from other cats, dogs or people, and occasionally from falling (see page 35). Signs of injury include *limping*, *bleeding* from a wound or from the nose, mouth or ears, grazes, breathing difficulty, unconsciousness or aggression when touched. Your vet will prescribe treatment depending on the injury, but it may include bandaging, a plaster cast, antibiotics and, in severe cases, amputation of a damaged limb. Recovery depends entirely on the nature of the injuries, but cats adapt very well to being on three legs. There is no way to prevent your cat from being injured, but indoor cats and those that only have access to an enclosed garden are less likely to be involved in accidents. Serious injuries, particularly where a bone may be broken, should always be treated as emergencies.

Itching

Mild itching from time to time is normal but moderate to severe itching is likely to be a sign of skin parasites, such as fleas (see page 84) or *ear mites*, or an allergy, especially if accompanied by scabs or bald patches. You should consult your vet to identify the problem.

Kidney failure

Kidney failure (or renal failure) usually occurs gradually as a result of ageing and is one of the most common health problems affecting middle-aged and older cats. It can also happen suddenly as a result of damage to the kidneys through trauma such as *poisoning* or infection. Signs vary but include increased *thirst*, increased urination, loss of appetite, weight loss, *vomiting*, lethargy, poor coat condition and bad breath. By the time most cats display these signs, three quarters of their kidney function has been damaged and there is no way to repair it. Vets often offer owners of older cats the option of having their cat tested at their yearly check-up: this cannot prevent kidney failure but early detection can extend life expectancy. A treated cat can live a relatively normal life for several years, but the kidneys will get worse over time and the cat may eventually need to be euthanased (see page 94).

Lice

Lice are small parasites that live on the cat's body. They are quite rare. They are passed from cat to cat but cat lice do not affect humans or other animals. If your cat has lice you will see little translucent eggs stuck to the hairs near his skin. He may scratch a little more than usual and may have scabs or dandruff. If infested, your vet will prescribe a suitable product to kill the lice. Treatment may take a few weeks but your cat should recover entirely. Dispose of his bedding and brushes but there is no need to treat the house. Some flea treatments stop adult lice from latching on to your cat, but will not affect any lice hatching from eggs already laid on his fur.

Limping

Consult your vet urgently if your cat is limping and is holding the limb at an odd angle, if there are wounds or if he is obviously in pain. If the limp is only slight and is not accompanied by any other signs of illness or distress, wait for a day to see if it improves and, if not, take him to a vet.

Being overweight can shorten your cat's natural life.

Obesity

Obesity is a serious condition that can lead to *diabetes*, *arthritis* and other weight-related illnesses. Cats can easily become overweight if they are fed too much or do not get enough exercise; because of this, obesity is more common in indoor-only cats. See pages 56–62 for information on how to feed your cat a proper diet. If you think your cat may be overweight, speak to your vet about putting him on a diet – you should never crash diet a cat.

Poisoning

Some common household substances are dangerous to your cat when they are eaten or when they

Foaming from the mouth can be a sign of poisoning.

make contact with his skin. They include things like paracetamol, permethrin (dog flea treatment), lilies and antifreeze – see pages 51 and 54 for more information. Cats tend to be good at avoiding poisons but they are not very resilient if they do come into contact with them.

Signs of poisoning vary greatly depending on the poison involved, but include *vomiting*, disorientation, foaming at the mouth, *convulsions*, swelling and skin irritation. Treatment also depends on the type of poison your cat has come into contact with, but it might involve aggressive fluid therapy (to wash out the system), induced vomiting or cleaning of the fur and skin. Your cat's recovery will depend on how much of the poison he came into contact with and how long it was before he got help. Most cats make a full recovery but, sadly, some cats suffer too much damage to their vital organs and die as a result.

Keep hazardous products such as bleach, antifreeze and lilies well out of reach of your cat and never give him medication meant for humans or other animals. If your cat is kept indoors all the time, make sure that you provide him with a safe, enriching environment so he does not chew out of boredom.

Renal failure

See *Kidney failure*.

Ringworm

Ringworm is not a worm but a fungal infection that invades the skin, hair or claws. Ringworm can affect other animals and people and is transferred by contact with an infected animal, object or environment. Ringworm is more likely to affect longhaired cats, old cats, young cats, ill cats or cats with fleas. Signs include *itching*, loss of hair through scratching, scabs on the skin and over-grooming.

Treatment involves antifungal medicine, shampoo or sprays, flea treatment (see page 84) and isolation. You may need to have your cat's fur cut short and you should

Ringworm has caused the sore patches on this kitten's skin.

stop grooming him to avoid spreading the spores of the fungus around the house. You will also need to decontaminate your house by vacuuming and disinfecting it. You should throw away any collars, bedding, brushes and soft toys that your cat has used and you should wear gloves when you touch your cat to avoid contracting ringworm yourself. Most cats respond to treatment within weeks and if you have only one cat it should be quite easy to manage the ringworm outbreak. In multi-cat households it can be harder to stop the infection spreading, but careful management should resolve it. In a very few cases the ringworm can be resistant to treatment. This is usually because the decontamination hasn't been carried out carefully enough or because the cat has a weak immune system. There is no way to prevent ringworm.

Roundworm

See page 85.

Sneezing or runny nose

Sneezing with a discharge from the nose may be related to one of the bacteria or viruses that cause *cat flu*. If your cat is vaccinated against cat flu, sneezes only occasionally and shows no other sign of illness, wait to see if the sneezing stops by itself as it may simply be an allergic reaction or mild infection. If it continues for a day or two, gets worse or other signs develop – breathing difficulties, weeping eyes, *coughing*, or blood or pus present in the discharge – visit your vet.

Sore teeth or gums

Consult your vet for advice, particularly if your cat is unwilling to eat or is pawing at his mouth: it may be a sign of *gingivitis and stomatitis*.

Stings

Wasp or bee stings are usually accompanied by a swelling and should resolve themselves within a few hours. Consult your vet if they do not go down after a few hours or if they occur around the mouth and throat as these could cause breathing difficulties.

Sunburn

Red, sore and/or bleeding around the tips of the ears or nose (particularly in white cats) can be signs of sunburn. Contact your vet for advice and try to keep your cat out of the sun or use a special cat suntan lotion or a baby suntan lotion on the tips of the ears and top of the nose in future. Do not put suntan lotion on broken skin.

Swellings

Swellings can be the result of many different things, including *stings*, tumours, *injuries* or abscesses. Consult your vet if your cat seems to be in pain or if the swelling persists for more than 24 hours. Do not try to treat the swelling yourself.

Sometimes *ticks* are mistaken for swellings. If your cat has a lump on his skin, check carefully to see whether it really is a swelling or whether it is a tick that should be removed.

Swollen belly

A swollen belly can be a sign of worms (see page 85), wet *FIP* or other illnesses. Consult your vet for advice.

Tapeworm

See page 85.

Thirst

A noticeable increase in thirst over several days should be investigated by your vet as it can be a sign of *diabetes* or kidney disease. If you have recently changed your cat from a wet diet to a dry diet, his thirst will increase naturally.

Ticks

Ticks are small, bloodsucking mites that are only about the size of a pinhead when they haven't fed but can grow up to a centimetre in size when full of blood. They live in rural environments such as grasses and woodlands, waiting for a host to pass by, and so are more common in cats that live in rural areas. If they are left untreated they can cause sores, infection and abscesses. Ticks, which are more common in mainland Europe and the USA than they are in the UK, can also transmit a number of different diseases. Ticks can spread Lyme disease, which, although rare, can be quite serious and can affect both you and your cat.

It is unlikely that you will notice that your cat has a tick until it becomes full with blood, at which point it may look like a lump or wart. It is best to take your cat to the vet to have a tick removed. If you want to remove it yourself, use tweezers to grasp it as close to your cat's skin as possible, then gently pull the tick out. Some vets also sell a special device, called a tick-remover, with which you can grasp the tick, twist and remove it. Be careful not to detach the tick's body from its head, which can then remain fixed in the skin and become infected. Do not try to burn the tick off. Ticks cause very little harm to your cat, but because they can transmit diseases it is always best to get rid of them.

Drinking more water than usual can be a sign of illness.

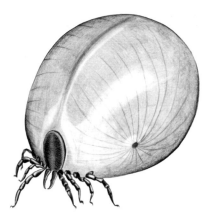

Some spot-on flea products available from your vet can prevent ticks as well as fleas and other parasites (see page 84).

Toileting problems

Straining to go to the toilet or toileting inappropriately in the house can be a sign of urinary tract disease. A male cat that strains to go to the toilet should be seen by a vet as a matter of urgency – see *Feline lower urinary tract disease (FLUTD)*.

Vomiting

Occasional vomiting is normal, particularly if the vomit is accompanied by hairballs. If the vomiting is severe, continues for over 24 hours or is accompanied by blood or other signs such as *diarrhoea*, then you should consult your vet.

Worms

See page 85.

Severe vomiting should be seen by a vet.

Giving your cat medicines

Many medicines are available in forms that are easier than tablets for a cat to take and for you to administer, such as **spot-ons** or **liquids**. When you do have to give your cat tablets, you can sometimes crush and mix them into strong-smelling food. However, some tablets have to be given whole and unless you can hide the tablet in a piece of meat – which many cats don't fall for – it is important that you are able to give them successfully.

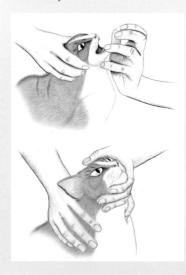

Tablets

1. First read the instructions carefully to make sure you are giving the medication properly.
2. If you have someone who can help, it will be much easier If they can hold your cat still as you give the pill.
3. If you are right-handed, hold your cat's head firmly with your left hand and tilt the head back gently so that the chin is in the air.
4. Take the tablet in between the thumb and forefinger of your right hand.
5. Use the middle finger of your right hand to lever your cat's jaw open.
6. Drop the tablet into the back of the throat.
7. Now let the mouth close and hold it shut with your left hand whilst keeping the chin in the air.
8. Use your right hand to stroke your cat's throat gently to encourage him to swallow.

Your cat may wriggle at first but you should be firm when holding him. It won't hurt him.

If you really struggle, you can get a tablet applicator from your vet. These hold the tablet at the end of a syringe-like applicator which can then be placed at the back of the throat and released. Try giving the tablet by hand first, though, as using an applicator like this is often no easier.

Other medicines

Spot-ons are applied to the back of the neck using a pipette. You should part the fur on the back of your cat's neck so you can apply the solution directly to the skin. Choose a point which is high enough to make it impossible for your cat to lick the medicine off.

Liquid medicines are squeezed (using a pipette or a plastic syringe) into the mouth for the cat to swallow. You should hold your cat as you would when giving a tablet and use your free hand to point the end of the pipette down and towards the inside of his cheek – do not point it directly down the throat. Squeeze gently so that the liquid squirts on to his cheek and dribbles down his throat. Once you have finished, close your cat's mouth, hold his chin up and stroke his throat to help him swallow.

AGEING AND DEATH

Cats have an average lifespan of between 14 and 16 years, although many live much longer. Because their lifespan is so much shorter than our own, most owners will, sadly, eventually have to deal with the ageing and death of their cat.

Signs of ageing

As your cat gets older, you may start to see some changes in the way he looks and behaves. These changes will be gradual and usually occur after the age of about 10.

As your cat gets older you may notice that he:

- Sleeps more than usual, and prefers to do this on soft, cushioned surfaces.
- Is less active and less inclined to play.
- Loses body condition and becomes more bony.
- Loses fur condition as he doesn't groom so often.
- Becomes more noisy as his hearing fades.
- Becomes a fussy eater as his sense of smell becomes less acute.

As well as these general signs of ageing, older cats are more prone to hyperthyroidism, kidney disease, diabetes and dementia (see pages 86–93). It is good to be aware of these conditions and to pay attention to your cat's habits so that you notice any changes quickly. Many vets offer to check for these diseases at a cat's yearly check-up and vaccination (see page 82), because early diagnosis can greatly increase your cat's length and quality of life.

WHEN TO VISIT A VET

You are the person most likely to notice changes in your cat because of your familiarity with his normal habits. You may see none of the signs mentioned below, but if you notice changes in your cat's behaviour that make you sufficiently concerned, contact the vet. If you have an older cat, take note if he:

- Wants to eat or drink noticeably more than usual (particularly if it is sudden).
- Loses interest in food or water.
- Becomes very quiet or withdrawn and/or does not want to move.
- Seems to be in pain if touched or is unable to sit comfortably.
- Shows no interest in grooming and has a poor coat condition.
- Has unexplained weight loss.
- Is suffering from toileting problems – incontinence, pain, frequent urination.
- Becomes aggressive when approached or touched.

Euthanasia

Although some cats die naturally in their own homes, most are eventually euthanased by a vet. While you may hear the terms 'put to sleep', 'put down' or 'humane destruction', euthanasia is the proper term for the process of ending a life painlessly – it translates as 'good death'. Making the decision to euthanase a cat is incredibly difficult for any owner but, if your vet recommends it, it is often the kindest option for a very sick or elderly cat.

Apart from severe injuries or disease, your vet may discuss euthanasia with you if, as a result of old age, your cat:

- Is unable to breathe comfortably.
- Cannot move or stand normally.
- Is unable to eat or drink properly.
- Is incontinent.
- Suffers from untreatable pain.

Your vet will talk over all the options with you and will only recommend euthanasia if he feels that your cat's quality of life will be very poor if you continue to attempt treatment.

WHAT WILL HAPPEN?

Once you have decided that euthanasia is the humane option, your vet will ask you to sign a consent form. You may be asked to decide between having the euthanasia carried out at home or in the surgery.

Most owners want to be with their cat when he dies, but your vet will understand if you do not feel that you can do this. It may be comforting for your cat to have someone familiar nearby, but if you are very distressed he may sense this and become anxious himself. Cats that are very uneasy may be sedated before the euthanasia to keep them calm.

Your vet will administer a fatal dose of a drug into one of your cat's veins using a needle. He will lose consciousness and his breathing and heartbeat will stop within seconds. He may take a final deep breath and there can be some involuntary movement of the muscles after death; his eyes will remain open. After death, your cat's muscles will relax completely, which may result in him soiling himself or baring his teeth. This can be upsetting because it may look as though he is scared or in pain, but it is only the muscles relaxing.

If your elderly cat is very reluctant to move over a number of days, and doesn't want to get up to eat or go to the toilet, you should take him to the vet.

After death

Most people choose either burial or cremation for their pet's remains. Your vet will discuss both options with you and can help to organize your wishes, or you can arrange it yourself.

BURIAL

Burial – where your cat's body is interred in the ground – can be carried out in a private pet cemetery or in your own garden.

Home burial

The majority of people choose to bury their cat at home in the garden, as this is the more personal and economical way. If you want to do this, you should bury your cat at least a metre below the surface and place a heavy rock or object on the dug ground to deter scavengers. You do not need permission from your Local Authority.

Private pet cemetery

If you wish to have your cat buried in a cemetery, ask your vet, search the internet or contact the Association of Private Pet Cemeteries and Crematoria to find details of one near you. Pet cemeteries offer a range of caskets and memorial plaques or headstones for you to choose from and will carry out a memorial service for your cat. Depending on the cemetery, you will be given a choice of two burial options:
- Individual burial – where there is a distinct plot in which your cat is buried.
- Communal burial – where a number of pets are buried together in an area of land but there is no individual plot.

You can deliver your cat's body to the pet cemetery, but many cemeteries also offer a collection service from your home or from the veterinary surgery. The cost of burial at a private pet cemetery depends on how you choose to bury your cat, where in the country you live and what sort of casket and headstone you purchase. Prices range from around £150 up to £350 and there is often an annual maintenance charge of up to £20 to pay for the upkeep of the grounds.

CREMATION

Cremation – where your cat's body is reduced to ash via a burning process – can only be done at a special crematorium. Ask your vet, search the internet or contact the Association of Private Pet Cemeteries and Crematoria to find details of one near you. Depending on the crematorium, you will be offered one of three options:
- Individual cremation – where your cat is cremated alone and the ashes are returned to you to scatter or keep.
- Communal cremation – where your cat is cremated with others and the ashes are scattered or buried in a garden of remembrance.
- Separated cremation – where your cat is cremated with others but the ashes are kept as separate as possible and are returned to you.

You can deliver your cat's body to the crematorium but most will collect from your vet and return the ashes to you if that is your wish. The cost of cremation depends on which service option you choose, where in the country you live and what sort of urn and/or memorial plaque you purchase. Prices range from around £30 up to £150.

ALTERNATIVE OPTIONS

There are a number of alternative options for a loved pet's body. These include:
- Donating the body to veterinary science – speak to your vet about this option.
- Creating a diamond – using your cat's ashes to make a diamond is a very new and expensive method of remembering a pet; it is now available in the UK.
- Preserving the body – it is possible (although rarely done in the UK) to freeze-dry, freeze or stuff pets.

Coping with loss

Everyone reacts differently to the loss of a pet; some go through intense feelings of loneliness or guilt while others just feel sad for some time. It is quite normal to be upset, and your vet will not think you are silly if you cry or show other emotions.

It can be hard to explain to children what has happened to their cat, but being honest is usually the best approach. Be careful about using terms like 'went away' or 'put to sleep' because these can be very confusing. It can help if children are involved in the process of saying goodbye – seeing the body and burial, or scattering the ashes, can help them to understand and get over their loss.

If you find it very difficult to recover from the loss of a pet, you may want to contact the Blue Cross Pet Bereavement Helpline or your GP. Details of the Blue Cross scheme can be found in the contact section of this book, page 126.

YOUR HEALTH

It is very rare for a human to catch something from their cat, just as it is very rare for a cat to catch something from a human, but it does happen from time to time.

Catching diseases from your cat

Infectious diseases that can be passed between humans and cats are called **zoonoses**. They can be transferred through direct contact with an infected cat's faeces or saliva, or through food or water that has been contaminated. Zoonoses are usually more of a nuisance than a serious threat to human health. However, certain people – those with weak immune systems, such as babies or people suffering from AIDS – will be more susceptible to serious infection.

Information on specific zoonoses appears below, but there are some general guidelines that will help prevent the transfer of infectious disease, including:

- Washing your hands after gardening, cleaning a litter tray and handling your cat.
- Wearing gloves when gardening or cleaning a litter tray.
- Keeping your cat healthy through annual check-ups and preventative healthcare (see page 82).
- Keeping both your and your cat's environment clean, including washing bedding, clearing litter trays daily and not allowing your cat on kitchen surfaces or dining tables.
- Feeding your cat either thoroughly cooked or commercial food.
- Seeking prompt veterinary attention should your cat seem unwell.

BITES

Cats do have bacteria in their mouths and, if you are bitten, it is possible for the wound to become infected. Clean any bites carefully and seek advice from your GP if there is any sign of infection such as swelling or pus.

CAT SCRATCH DISEASE

On rare occasions, bacteria on a cat's claws can get into a scratch wound and cause cat scratch disease. It usually leads only to swollen lymph nodes (often in the neck and under the arms) but it can cause other flu-like symptoms. The affected person normally recovers quickly but more serious illness can occur, particularly in people with weak immune systems.

Although it is common for adult cats to carry the bacteria, cat scratch disease occurs most often through a kitten scratch. Don't teach your kitten to play with people's hands or feet and don't let children play roughly with cats or kittens. Fleas can transfer the bacteria from one cat to another, so keeping your cat flea-free will reduce the chance of his carrying the disease – see page 84 for more information.

FLEAS

Cat fleas don't live on humans but they can bite and irritate the skin. If swallowed, it is also possible for a flea to transfer worms (see page 85). Proper flea treatment will keep your house flea-free – see page 84.

RABIES

Most cat viruses cannot be passed to humans, but it is possible for a cat with rabies to infect a human through a bite. This is not a problem in the UK, where there is no rabies, but in the US and other countries you should vaccinate your cat against rabies and consult a doctor when bitten by any animal.

RINGWORM

A cat infected with ringworm (see page 91) releases fungal spores into the environment and these can infect a human, particularly if they get into a break in the skin, such as a scratch. Symptoms in humans include patches of round, ring-shaped itchy skin and areas of hair loss. The condition is easily treated but this should be done as soon as possible to avoid re-infection, and your cat should also be treated immediately. Isolating your pet in one room while he is treated and avoiding direct contact with him and his belongings will help to contain the condition.

A red, ring-shaped mark on the skin is a sign of ringworm infection.

SALMONELLA

Humans usually catch salmonella through food rather than from cats, but you can contract the bacterial infection through infected faeces. The most common symptom is diarrhoea and the infection usually clears up over a matter of days with rest and plenty of liquid. Good hygiene, such as washing your hands after handling your cat or his litter tray, will help prevent infection.

Children

Zoonoses affect children more often than adults because children are more likely to touch faeces accidentally, when playing in a garden or sandpit or when playing with a cat. Carefully treating your cat for fleas and worms (see pages 84 and 85), covering sandpits and teaching children good hygiene – washing hands and not putting fingers in mouths – will help reduce the chance of infection.

Hygiene is important for your, and your cat's, health.

TOXOPLASMOSIS

This is a common condition caused by a parasite that can be carried by any animal and there are many different ways that you can become infected, one of which is through your cat. Cats become infected with the parasite only once – usually through hunting. They remain infectious for a few weeks before becoming immune. However, the cysts that the cat releases in his faeces during this time can remain infectious for months and can be transferred to a human through direct contact.

Around one third of the UK population has had toxoplasmosis and become immune before the age of 30; the symptoms are so mild that most people don't know they have had it. However, if a woman who isn't immune through prior contact with the parasite becomes infected when pregnant, she will be at risk of miscarriage or other birth complications. Fortunately, this is very rare because cats are infectious for such a short period and because, with a little care, it is easy to avoid any contact with the parasite. If you are pregnant and own a cat, you should:

- Make sure that the litter tray is cleaned regularly because faeces become infectious only after they have been around for 24 hours.
- Ask someone else to change cat litter, or wear gloves and an apron when doing it.
- Avoid gardening but, if you must, use gloves and wash your hands carefully afterwards.
- Wash your hands after handling raw meat and cook it thoroughly before eating.
- Wash fruit, vegetables and salads before eating them.
- Avoid cured (smoked) meats and unpasteurized dairy products.
- On a farm, don't handle lambing ewes or newborn lambs, or the clothing of anyone involved in lambing.

WORMS

Roundworms and tapeworms are parasites that live in the intestines. They rarely cause symptoms and are often noticed only because worms or worm segments appear in the stool of the infected person. You are very unlikely to become infected, even if your cat does have worms. However, proper worming and good hygiene will reduce this possibility even further. See page 85.

Allergies

Some people have an allergic reaction when they come into contact with a cat. Having an allergy to cats doesn't necessarily mean that you cannot live with a cat, but it does depend on the severity of your reaction.

An allergic reaction to cats is caused by a protein in their saliva and skin – not their fur – called Fel d 1.

The symptoms of an allergic reaction range from mildly itchy eyes and a runny nose to a severe skin rash or asthma attack. If you or a member of your family is suffering a severe reaction to your cat, you should contact your GP immediately. However, if your reaction is only mild to moderate, there are a number of different actions that you can take to ease your symptoms, including:

- Keeping your cat out of bedrooms.
- Keeping your house clean, vacuumed and swept, particularly in areas where your cat sleeps.
- Washing your cat's bedding regularly.
- Grooming your cat outside and wiping him down with a damp cloth.
- Using an allergen-reducing product such as Bio-Life PetalCleanse around your house or on your cat.
- Talking to your doctor about therapies and antihistamine products that can reduce your allergic reaction to a much more comfortable level.
- Repeating and increasing exposure to the same cat or cats – this can reduce an allergy-sufferer's sensitivity over time.

HYPOALLERGENIC CATS

A company in the United States has created cats that apparently do not cause allergic reactions. The cats, which cost between $6,000 and $31,000, are selectively bred so that they do not produce the Fel d 1 protein that causes the allergic reaction in some humans. Animal welfare organizations have expressed concern over this kind of mass commercialization of pet breeding, particularly when there are so many homeless cats in the world.

If you sneeze every time you are near a cat you may be allergic.

There are numerous claims that certain breeds (e.g. the Devon Rex or Sphynx – see pages 19 and 21) or colours of cats are better for allergy sufferers than others, but no scientific studies have found these claims to be true. It is the case that some people find they are more allergic to one cat than another, but this has more to do with the individual cat and the person's level of built-up immunity to that particular cat than to any colour or breed type.

INSURANCE

When you take out pet insurance you pay a monthly or yearly premium in return for financial help with vet bills when you need it. Your cat may be lucky enough to go through life with very few health problems, but if he does fall victim to an unexpected illness or injury, pet insurance can potentially save you thousands of pounds. Around 1.8 million pet insurance claims are made each year in the UK, but many more owners struggle with vet bills that they cannot afford because they have no insurance.

Types of policy

Policies vary greatly from one to the other and it is not always the case that the higher the premium you pay the better the cover you get. Insurance providers often state high figures, such as '£5,000 vet fees covered', but it is vitally important that you read the small print because they often put limitations on these figures.

There are three main types of insurance available:

Policies with fee limits, condition limits and time limits

These policies limit both the length of time and how much money you can claim for each condition.

Example: The policy may cover up to £5,000 vet fees but there is a limit of £1,000 per condition and you can claim only for a 12-month period after the condition is first noticed. A policy like this will not cover your cat for long-term conditions that last beyond a year or that cost over £1,000 to treat. Because of the limited cover they offer, they tend to have the lowest premiums.

Policies with fee limits and condition limits but no time limits

These policies limit how much money you can claim for each condition, but as long as you renew your policy each year there is no limit on how long you can claim for.

Example: You can claim up to £5,000 per condition with no time limit as long as you renew your policy each year, but once you reach your fee limit you cannot claim for that particular condition again. The cost of the premiums for this type of policy depends entirely on the fee limit of the policy – the lower the fee limit the lower the premium.

Policies with a yearly fee limit, sometimes called 'lifetime' policies

These policies have a fee limit per year and there are no limits per condition.

Example: You can claim £5,000 in vet fees each and every year you remain with the insurer with no other limits. These policies provide extensive cover for both long- and short-term illnesses but the premiums do tend to be higher than the other policy types.

Taking out insurance means that you will be prepared if the worst happens.

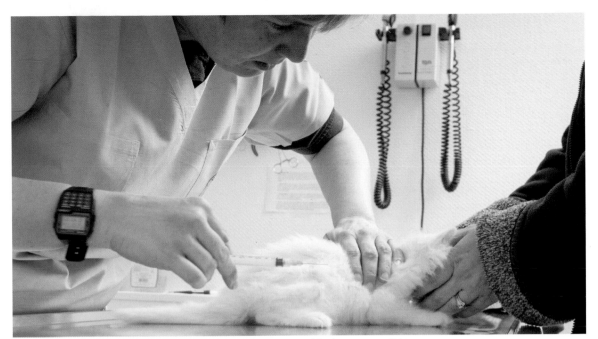

Routine veterinary treatment, such as vaccinations, is not covered by insurance policies.

Check your policy

Be sure that you understand all the conditions of a policy before you agree to it.

Exclusions

Exclusions are the things that are not covered in the policy (e.g. routine treatments such as neutering and vaccinations). Neither do cat insurance policies usually cover the cost of dental work or third party liability (insurance against the cost of compensation for any third party who comes to harm or has property damaged due to the actions of your cat). If you do want to be covered for these, check that they are included.

Pre-existing conditions

Most insurance companies will not pay for treatment of a condition that your cat had before the insurance was taken out. This means that if your cat develops a long-term illness when he is not insured, you will not be able to take out insurance later on to cover that illness. Simply 'forgetting' to mention a pre-existing condition when you take out the policy is not a good idea, as your entire insurance policy will become void if the insurance provider becomes suspicious.

Excesses

The excess is the amount of each claim you must pay before your insurer pays the rest. Excesses vary from a £50 flat fee up to 50 per cent of the final bill.

Example: Your cat may need an operation costing £3,000. If you have a policy with a fixed fee excess of £50, you will have to pay £50 and your insurer will pay £2,950.

If you have a policy with a 50 per cent excess, you will have to pay £1,500 and your insurer will pay £1,500. If you have no policy, you will have to pay £3,000.

As a rule, the larger the excess you pay, the smaller your premiums will be. You may have the option of increasing the amount of excess you pay to reduce your premiums.

Additional cover

Apart from covering the cost of vet fees, most insurance policies offer cover for other eventualities. These may include:

Advertising and reward – the cost of advertising and offering a reward for a lost cat.
Holiday cancellation – the cost of a holiday that has to be cancelled due to your cat's serious illness.
Hospitalization – the cost of putting your cat in a cattery should you be taken into hospital.
Death – the cost of euthanasia and cremation.

On the whole, these additional covers are not very useful to most cat owners. You should base your decision to buy a policy on the vet fee cover first and foremost.

Premium

Premiums vary according to a range of different factors, including your cat's age, pedigree, medical history and your postcode, but are usually somewhere between £10 and £30 a month. You can often reduce this by applying online, increasing your excess or insuring more than one pet with a single insurer. Also, don't forget to haggle; insurers will often match each other's prices to get your custom.

Chapter 5

YOUR CAT'S BEHAVIOUR

The key to preventing behaviour problems is to socialize a kitten properly when he is young and to provide a happy life for your cat – as described in Chapter 3 – so that he becomes a well-balanced adult. Behaviour problems usually occur when this balance is lost, often through stress, illness or trauma.

Behaviour problems are usually just natural behaviours that are taken to extremes by an unbalanced cat to comfort himself. For example, a balanced cat may spray urine around the outskirts of his territory, but a stressed cat can bring this into his house – not a normal place for a cat to spray and very upsetting for the average owner. Behaviour problems can impact greatly on the relationship between a cat and his owner, creating an atmosphere of stress and anxiety that in turn can worsen the problem. It is best to deal with any behaviour problems as soon as they arise.

BEHAVIOUR PROBLEMS

There are two sides to any behaviour problem – the cause and the problem itself. Both need to be resolved at the same time, otherwise the problem will simply surface again in a different form. In seeking to prevent and solve any behaviour problem, it is vital that at all times you observe the following:

Golden rules
- **Neuter your cat. This can be the solution to many territorially and sexually related behaviour problems.**
- **Never punish your cat aggressively with smacking, angry shouting or chasing. If you do, it is likely to cause your cat to repeat the behaviour more often for one of two reasons: you have made him more stressed and anxious; he has found that doing it gets your attention.**

Common causes

If your cat is showing one of the behaviour problems described on pages 102–107, you will need to think about the possible causes (see below) at the same time as treating the problem. The causes of all behaviour problems usually fall into one of just a few categories.

ILLNESS

Any change in behaviour – particularly if it is sudden – can be a sign of ill health, so you should always speak to a vet before you do anything else.

OVERCROWDING AND BULLYING

Too many animals in one space – in your home or in the neighbourhood – can lead to bullying and stress over territory or resources. It will help if you:
- Increase resources (litter trays, feeding places, sleeping places and cat flaps) to avoid competition in the house.
- Place key resources in a number of different locations so timid cats can use them in peace.
- Reduce contact with stray or neighbours' cats – use secure fencing/hedging around your garden, install a cat flap that allows only your own cat to enter the house (see page 50) and use net curtains so your cat cannot see the 'competition' out of the window.
- Don't add more cats to an already harmonious multi-cat household.
- Neuter all your house pets – this can reduce territorial aggression, lower stress levels and will avoid attracting other cats into your home.
- Rehome a pet – this is a very hard decision to make, but if you have tried everything else and your cat is still suffering stress due to crowded living conditions, it may be the best option.

LACK OF SECURITY

Cats are creatures of routine and if that routine is changed suddenly, feelings of insecurity can manifest themselves as a behaviour problem. Moving house or the arrival of a new baby may be enough to trigger a behaviour problem. It will help if you introduce your cat to new things and changes gradually.

LACK OF STIMULATION

Indoor-only cats and those with very few opportunities for human interaction, play and carrying out natural behaviours will store up excess energy which may give rise to a behaviour problem. Some individual cats and certain breeds will have more energy than others. If you are considering a pedigree cat, make sure you do your research because some, such as the Siamese, are often high-maintenance and may require more patience and attention. It will help if you:
- Give your cat outside access.
- Neuter your cat to remove the instinct to go in search of mates and breed.
- Provide your cat with plenty of toys, scratching posts, climbers and cat grass to enrich his indoor environment – see pages 50–51 for information on creating a perfect indoor environment for your cat.
- Play more games with your cat, hide food around the house and use puzzle feeders to burn up excess energy and create interest at meal times.

Outdoor activities such as hunting, climbing and eating grass must be given an outlet if your cat is kept inside.

OVER-DEPENDENCE OR ATTENTION-SEEKING

Too much attention and spoiling (e.g. if you feed from the table, let your cat sleep in your bedroom or get up in the night to let him out) can lead both to an increase in attention-seeking behaviour and to stress over small changes, such as if you need to spend more time away from home or if a relative comes to live with you. It will help if you:

- Ignore your cat when he is demanding attention – give it only when he is calm.
- Don't reward the behaviour problem by reacting to it – an attention-seeking cat will relish any attention, good or bad.
- Don't spoil your cat – making certain rooms off-limits and not allowing him to have food from the table will give him boundaries and ultimately make him more balanced.
- Distract him from focusing on you – ask other family members or friends to spend time with him and use puzzle feeders and toys to keep him busy and use up energy.
- Give your cat outside access – a boring environment can lead to over-dependence on the only source of interest available to him: you.

TRAUMA

A traumatic experience (from your cat's point of view) can cause a behaviour problem – e.g. a dog chasing your cat may lead to reluctance to go outside, or a set of car keys crashing to the floor at the wrong time may lead to reluctance to use the litter tray. It will help if you:

- Move resources to new locations that are not associated with the traumatic event.
- Create a more secure environment by enclosing gardens and covering windows.

If you are struggling with a problem, try pheromone sprays or call on the services of a feline behaviourist to help you – see page 107 for more on these options.

Common problems

You should always deal with the cause and the problem together. All the causes outlined above can lead to the following problems.

URINE-SPRAYING INDOORS

Spraying is a natural territorial marking behaviour that any cat – male or female, neutered or not – may do. It should not be confused with toileting.

When a cat sprays, he stands backed-up to a vertical object, such as a tree trunk or fence post, and sprays a short burst of urine on to it. The marks are used by the cat to make an area smell more familiar, as a reminder of where his territory is not secure and as a message to any passing cats that they are entering occupied territory, or (in the case of un-neutered cats) that there is a potential mate or competitor nearby.

A cat will very rarely spray inside his own house because this territory, where he eats and sleeps, is secure. If your cat does spray indoors, it is a sign that something, from his point of view, is wrong. Common causes often include competition from new animals or people, or a sudden change in normal routine.

When a cat sprays, it is very unpleasant for anyone who lives in the house and so can put a lot of pressure on your relationship with your cat. It is essential that you deal with the problem as soon as possible because the longer a cat sprays, the more likely he is to continue.

Address the cause

See the common causes of behaviour problems listed on pages 101–102. If any of these might be affecting your cat, you will need to deal with it at the same time as the spraying.

Clues can be found in the location and timing of your cat's spraying behaviour. If it is near windows or entrances and exits to your home, then it could be something outside that is upsetting him. If it is in corridors or on internal doors, then he is probably bothered by something inside the house. If he repeatedly sprays in the same room but nowhere else, it may be a trauma that he experienced at that location. If he does it only when you go away for the weekend, it could be insecurity caused by being left with a petsitter he is not familiar with.

If your cat is backing up to household objects, raising a quivering tail and spraying a short burst of urine on to vertical objects, he is marking his territory rather than urinating.

If your cat squats with his tail low and leaves a large puddle of urine or faeces on a horizontal surface, he is toileting rather than spraying.

Clean it up

It is important to clean the sprayed area properly so that your cat doesn't re-spray there later. There are five steps to doing this effectively:

- Dab the area with absorbent kitchen towel.
- Scrub it with a suitable cleaning solution – either 2 tablespoons of biological washing powder mixed with quarter of a litre of water, or a special cat-urine cleaner available from pet shops and supermarkets. Do not use bleach because, like urine, it contains ammonia and will only encourage your cat to spray the same area again.
- Dab the area with absorbent kitchen towel.
- Spray surgical spirit on to the area using a plant mister – for delicate fabrics test this on a small area first.
- Dab the area with absorbent kitchen towel.

Dispose of the waste carefully and wash your hands thoroughly.

Deny access

Do not allow your cat access to the cleaned site for a while – at least for a week but for longer if possible. If a cat can sense a fading scent mark, he will instinctively want to 'top it up'. If you cannot stop him from getting to the site, try putting his food bowl in the same place as this may deter him.

TOILETING INDOORS

The majority of cats go to the toilet in a litter tray or in the garden. It is unusual for a cat not to use a litter tray when inside his own home, so it usually signals a problem.

When a cat urinates or defecates, he squats and does it on a horizontal surface, usually in a private area. If your cat is urinating on vertical objects, such as walls or doors in exposed areas, it is likely that he is spraying rather than urinating – see page 102.

Common causes of a cat urinating in his own home include illness, fear, or too much competition for resources. As with spraying, it is very important to deal with the problem as soon as possible to prevent it becoming a habit.

Address the cause

See the common causes of behaviour problems listed on pages 101–102. If any of these might be affecting your cat, you will need to deal with it at the same time as the house-soiling.

As well as the more common causes, you should also consider your cat's age. Elderly cats who find it difficult to move may struggle to get to a litter tray in time.

Litter-tray problems

House-soiling may happen if your cat finds the litter or litter tray you have provided for him unsuitable. Ask yourself the following questions:

- How many litter trays do you have in the house – do you have one per cat plus one extra?
- How often do you clean out the litter trays – are they done every day as soon as the urine or faeces is noticed?
- Where are the litter trays – have you tried other secluded positions?
- What types of trays are used – have you tried different styles?
- Have you tried a different type of litter?
- Are you using scented litter or tray liners – it may smell nice to you, but does it smell nice to your cat?

For more detailed information on providing the right litter and tray, see pages 64–65.

Clean it up

Clean the soiled area in the same way as you would clean a sprayed area – see above.

Deny access

Once it is cleaned, stop your cat from returning to the area where he soiled for at least a week, or longer if possible. Move furniture over the spot or if need be place his food bowl on it to deter him from soiling there again.

House-soiling problems can occur if you do not provide your cat with the right kind of litter tray or litter.

This solid and sturdy scratching post is ideal for these kittens, but it will not be tall enough for them when they grow up and they may look for alternative surfaces.

SCRATCHING INDOORS

Cats scratch to leave marks for themselves and other cats, and to keep their claws in good condition. They usually make their scratch marks outside on objects in prominent positions and on scratching posts in the home.

If your cat scratches on your furniture or doors, it may be because he does not have enough opportunity to keep his claws in good condition or because he does not feel secure in his own home. It is best to deal with indoor scratching as soon as possible, not least because of the cost of damage done to household objects.

Address the cause

See the common causes of behaviour problems listed on pages 101–102. If any of these might be affecting your cat, you will need to deal with it at the same time as the scratching.

As with spraying, where your cat scratches can be a clue to why he is doing it. If it is always near external doors and windows, something outside, such as a neighbour's cat, may be the problem, but if it is always near inner doorways and corridors then it could be something inside the house that is worrying him.

Scratching-post problems

A cat who is scratching indoors purely out of a lack of suitable scratching posts may stop as soon as you provide him with the scratching posts he needs. If he is scratching because of stress, providing the right type and number of scratching posts may help but don't forget that the stress will still be there and will be expressed

until it is dealt with. When looking at the scratching posts you provide, consider:
- How many do you have – are there enough for the number of cats you own?
- Where are they placed – would your cat prefer them in different positions?
- What type of posts are you using – have you tried different types and styles?
- Are the posts tall and sturdy enough – do they stand up well to a good scratching?

For more on scratching posts, see page 72.

Deter

To deter your cat from scratching a particular object, you need to cover the area in something that is unpleasant to scratch. Successful products include foil, double-sided tape (one that isn't too sticky), plastic sheeting or Perspex. Check the area each day to make sure that your deterrent is still in place and is working.

Distract

Once you have covered the area that is affected, place a sturdy scratching post nearby to attract your cat to this more appropriate surface. Make sure you replace like for like – for example, if your cat is scratching a carpet, make sure you get a low-lying scratcher with a material covering (e.g. sisal), but if he is scratching a doorframe use a vertical scratcher made from wood. Once your cat begins using his scratching post, you can gradually move it away from the original spot to a more suitable space.

AGGRESSION

Aggression is a complex problem and is hardly ever caused by a 'bad' cat. Aggression tends to be directed either towards humans or towards other pets and has a very damaging and disruptive effect on any household.

Address the cause

See the common causes of behaviour problems listed on pages 101–102. If any of these might be affecting your cat, you will need to deal with it at the same time as the aggression.

Other, more specific, reasons for aggression include:
- Pain/illness – a cat may lash out to defend himself when in pain, so it is worth repeating that in all cases of aggression you should first seek the advice of a vet.
- Redirection – a cat who is upset by one thing may lash out in frustration at something completely different: e.g. a cat who sees another cat through a window may strike out at a passing person in frustration at not being able to defend his territory.
- Predation – a cat who hunts things that aren't really prey, such as passing legs or other pets, may be doing so because he does not have sufficient outlet for his hunting instincts: e.g. a cat kept permanently inside.

A small amount of power play can be expected in a multi-cat household, but you may need to intervene if it becomes prolonged and vicious.

- Fear – a cat that lashes out to protect himself from a perceived threat (e.g. a feral cat) may attack a person trying to help him because he is afraid.
- Play – a cat who exhibits aggression by becoming over-excited and going one step too far when playing may be doing so because he was taken from his mother too young or has been encouraged to play roughly by an owner, and so has not been taught the boundaries between play and pain.
- Competition – a cat may attack another pet or person because he wants to be the dominant member of the group: for instance, a cat that was once the top cat in his owner's eyes but now feels under threat from a newcomer in the house, or a cat who shares his space with many other cats and feels insecure.

If you are not certain why your cat has become aggressive, you should seek the advice of a pet behaviourist (see page 107). In fact, this is such a complex and potentially dangerous problem, it can be difficult to resolve without help. The following advice can ease aggression but may not be enough on its own to solve the problem.

Ignore the cat

This can be difficult when your ankles are being ambushed with teeth and claws, or when two loved pets are at each other's throats, but shouting or running around increases stress levels and can only make a bad situation worse.

If your cat is being aggressive towards you when you are petting him, stand up and let him fall from your lap as soon as he goes too far. Do not lash out or shout, simply get up and walk away.

If you are being ambushed by your cat and it is impossible to ignore him, try wearing protective

clothing. Wearing wellies, gloves or thick clothing around the house may seem like an extreme measure, but, although your cat may try harder at first, if you can ignore his attacks for a while he may stop trying.

You can also make sure that your cat's claws are kept trimmed to reduce the chance of injury to you or to other animals in the house – see page 68.

Startle the cat

Clapping or using a plant mister or water pistol to spray a short burst of water on to an aggressive cat (not directly into the eyes) can also help to break the cycle and teach a cat not to attack. You must be consistent with this and try not to over-react by shouting or chasing.

If two cats are fighting and, having tried to ignore it, you feel you must break it up, don't chase after the cats. Instead, clap loudly and, if that fails, use a blanket to cover the cats. This will usually stop them, but if you do need to get involved to separate them it will also make sure that you are not caught in the crossfire.

Reward good behaviour

Never give your cat attention when he is being aggressive (this includes negative attention such as shouting angrily and lashing out). When he is calm and sociable give him a treat.

Deter

If the aggression is born out of frustration or boredom, making a cat's environment more exciting can help to reduce aggressive tendencies – see page 101. When playing with your cat, use a toy that is on the end of a stick or string so your hands are not in the firing line. If you do not let your cat outside, consider giving him access to your garden to help release pent-up energy and allow a more natural lifestyle.

Make a diary

Take note of whom your cat attacks, when and where the attacks occur, what your cat was doing before the attack and any other factors that you think may give clues to the reasoning behind aggression. This information will be invaluable to a behaviourist should you need to call one.

Wearing wellies around the house may seem like a strange idea, but it can make all the difference to an attention-seeking ambushing cat.

ANXIETY

Some cats are more timid than others simply because it is part of their character. It can be difficult for us to deal with anxious cats, particularly because we often get a cat for affection and may find it unrewarding to own a nervous cat. However, many owners of initially nervous cats who have worked through the problems find that they develop a very rewarding and strong relationship with their pet.

Address the cause

See the common causes of behaviour problems listed on pages 101–102. If any of these might be affecting your cat, you will need to deal with it at the same time as the nervousness. Although other reasons may be involved, anxiety tends to be due to one of three factors: it could be a character trait; a lack of contact with humans and family life during the key socialization period (up to 12 weeks old); or a traumatic experience.

Avoid confrontation

Think about how you communicate with your cat – see pages 41–42. Don't confront him or use aggressive behaviour, such as staring or directly approaching him. Remember that what *you* think is normal and affectionate may appear threatening to him. Don't force him to come out of hiding places.

Create a safe haven

Make sure your house provides plenty of quiet, hidden and high spots for your cat to get some peace away from people and other animals.

Be patient

Take time to introduce yourself gently. Sit in the same room as your cat and do something quiet like reading a book, sleeping or drawing. Gradually increase the time you spend with him without pressurizing him.

Let him make the first move, but if he approaches you don't suddenly stick your hand out or go to grab him. You can encourage him out of a hiding place by

If you read quietly in the same room as your cat, his curiosity may well get the better of him.

feeding him while you are in the room. Put the food down, walk away and sit down facing away from the food so that he doesn't feel as if you are watching him.

Once your cat is brave enough to stay out of hiding and approach you, continue to be calm and quiet around him and always allow him to initiate contact. Everyday things such as vacuuming may be very stressful for him, so avoid exposing him to these anxieties by putting him away in a quiet room while you vacuum the rest of the house. Also, you will need to take special care at particular times of the year, such as bonfire night or Christmas, when there may be fireworks going off or a lot of noisy strangers around your house.

OVER-GROOMING

Over-grooming is when a cat grooms himself (licks, bites or chews) over and over, often in the same few locations. It can cause bald patches and sores.

Address the cause

It may be possible for you and your cat to live with mild over-grooming but the habit is often the result of one of the common causes of behaviour problems – see pages 101–102 – and so should be dealt with to avoid worsening the problem. Usually over-grooming is stress- or health-related.

Examine your cat's diet

Look at what you feed your cat. A poor diet can result in a poor coat and skin condition. Try an alternative diet with a different nutritional balance – see pages 56–60 for more on nutrition.

Check for fleas and other parasites

Over-grooming may be a result of a parasite infestation or allergy. Check that you are carrying out a proper preventative health routine and that the products you are using are effective. See page 84 for advice.

Make sure your timid cat is given plenty of opportunity to hide when he is feeling insecure; over time he will become braver.

EATING NON-EDIBLE ITEMS

When a cat sucks, chews or eats items that are not edible – e.g. leather, wool or plastic – it is called **pica**. It can be mild, where a cat likes to suck a woollen jumper once in a while, or it can be severe, where whole leather sofas are destroyed and large quantities of leather are swallowed.

Pica tends to be more common in Siamese and other oriental breeds, as well as in kittens between two and eight months old and cats that have no outdoor access.

Address the cause

See the common causes of behaviour problems listed on pages 101–102. If any of these might be affecting your cat, you will need to deal with it at the same time as the pica.

Examine your cat's diet

Look at what you feed your cat to make sure that he is not compensating for a poor diet. Try an alternative diet with increased fibre content – see pages 56–60 for more on nutrition. Cats that are kept indoors all the time may appreciate food more akin to a 'natural' diet, such as whole rodent or chick carcasses – these can be purchased from shops that supply reptile food.

Deter

Bitter apple or eucalyptus (Olbas) oil can be added to items that are likely to come under attack to make them less appealing to your cat. If it is possible to put favoured items out of the way, it can help to reduce the

Grooming is natural and healthy but it can become a behaviour problem if the cat grooms excessively to reassure himself.

damage. However, if the original cause is not dealt with, the behaviour is likely to appear in another form.

Distract

Make your cat's indoor environment more stimulating and try to distract him from his usual habit by giving him more interesting objects to chew. Cooked meat bones, rawhide chews, pig's-ear chews or chewable cat or dog toys may be used; also try giving him his dinner in a puzzle feeder or in a timer feeder that dispenses food throughout the day to distract him. If your cat is chewing plants, make sure he has access to cat grass (see page 50).

Therapies

There are a number of other options that may help you deal with your cat's behaviour problem but it is important to realize that pheromone sprays and drug therapies are not solutions in themselves. They will succeed only if used in conjunction with the behaviour-altering techniques described in this chapter or prescribed by a professional behaviourist.

Pheromone therapy

A cat's feelings of security in his home environment are backed up by the familiar smells of 'home'. This includes the smell of you and your family, but also the scent marks that he himself leaves when he rubs his head on furniture, doors or corners around your house. These marks are the natural way for a cat to leave messages for himself to say that his territory is secure and safe.

When a cat does not feel secure and safe in his home it can lead to the development of a behaviour problem as he tries to leave warning signals about his insecurity and ward off potential threats. To try to combat these feelings of insecurity you can buy ready-made synthetic cat pheromones to spray around your house to convince your cat that the environment is safe.

These pheromones are called Feliway and Felifriend and they are available as plug-in diffusers and sprays.

On their own they are not enough to cure a cat suffering with a behaviour problem, but they can be a helpful addition to a treatment programme.

Drug therapy

Medications aimed at reducing stress are a relatively recent development in veterinary medicines. They are similar to antidepressants, are used only in the most desperate cases and are effective only if used in conjunction with the other treatment programmes. You should talk to your vet about whether your cat would be a suitable candidate for this type of therapy.

Cat behaviourists

When nothing seems to work or you feel unable to deal with a behaviour problem, it's always best to call in the experts before you let it go too far. Your vet will be able to refer you to a reliable cat behaviourist, who will come to your house and make a proper assessment of your cat's behaviour, his relationship with you and your other pets, and any recent events that may have caused the problem.

The behaviourist will then devise a plan of action for you to follow to help you retrain your cat and introduce the necessary changes to his life to make him feel more secure and balanced.

Chapter 6

BREEDING FROM YOUR CAT

If you are considering breeding from your cat, the first question you must ask yourself is, why?

Breeding is time-consuming, expensive and of no benefit to the cats involved – or to the hundreds of thousands of unwanted cats and kittens that need homes already. Periods of continuous observation, taking time off work and feeding every few hours throughout the day and night for several weeks may be required. The cost of raising kittens is enormous. Food costs will be at least double for three months; vaccinations for a litter of six can be as much as £600 and vet bills will also increase dramatically through the cost of treating the kittens for fleas (see page 84) and worming them (see page 85), as well as having the vet visit your home after the birth to check over both mother and kittens. If you intend to breed pedigrees, you should also add the cost of extra vaccinations for the mother cat before mating, the stud fee and the cost of registering each kitten as pedigree.

The best advice is to get your cat neutered without delay – see page 81 for more information on the health and welfare benefits. Having said that, this book covers the basics of breeding simply because you may find yourself in a position of having to look after a pregnant or nursing cat by chance and it is helpful to know what to expect.

YOUR PREGNANT CAT

Most cats manage their own pregnancies without any help from their human owners. However, there are a few key points that you must consider, including the correct feeding of a pregnant cat and what to do should anything go wrong.

Mating

Both male and female cats can be sexually active from just four months old. If the conditions are right (i.e. if there is enough light and warmth), until she is mated an un-neutered female cat will come into heat for a period of two to three weeks, and may then only have a two-week break before she comes into heat again. When in heat, cats usually become affectionate, attention-seeking and noisy. They roll around on the floor, raise their rear quarters and knead the floor over and over. Tom cats from miles around will attempt to reach the female by any means necessary, even if this means breaking into your home! If they cannot reach her, she will attempt to escape to reach them.

When cats are very young, they may display no signs of being in heat. As a result, many owners are taken by surprise when they find their six-month-old kitten giving birth to kittens of her own. The only safe way to prevent pregnancy is to get all cats neutered before they become sexually active. If you have male and female cats and kittens – even if they are related – they will mate with each other unless they are neutered.

Once the tom cat has reached a female in heat he will repeatedly mate with her over 24 hours. Each time he will mount her, bite her neck and then release her. As he releases her, barbs on his penis tear the vagina and induce ovulation – she will turn and lash out at him each time.

Cats mate repeatedly, but each mating takes only seconds.

After mating, a female cat will remain in heat for 24–48 hours. During this time she may be mated by another tom cat – it is possible for a female cat to have a litter of kittens that is fathered by two different toms.

Once a cat has given birth, it can take just 48 hours before she is in heat and able to get pregnant again: the domestic cat is one of the world's most prolific breeders.

Pregnancy

Pregnancy lasts for nine weeks. A vet can confirm pregnancy from three weeks, but will be unable to give an accurate delivery date unless the mating date is known.

A cat may show some behavioural changes during pregnancy, such as increased affection, irritability or vomiting, but the main changes will be the increase in the size of her appetite and her belly.

FEEDING A PREGNANT CAT

A pregnant cat will eat at least 50 per cent more food than normal. From the last few weeks of pregnancy up until she stops nursing her kittens, her appetite will double. By the time the kittens are born, the mother cat should be free-fed a specialized high-energy kitten food. Gradually change her over to this in the last few weeks of her pregnancy to ensure she gets the extra nutrients needed to sustain herself and her kittens. Fresh water should be available at all times.

Birth

It is best to keep a cat indoors from the eighth week of her pregnancy because she will begin to seek somewhere warm, dry and dark to give birth to her kittens.

Position a kittening box in a suitable location. This can be made from cardboard or purchased for anything from £15 to £200 from pet shops. You should line the base with something soft and cover that with plenty of layers of clean, absorbent, disposable material – kitchen towel is ideal.

The beginning of labour is signalled by nervousness, panting, pacing or rolling. For approximately 24 hours before labour, a cat's temperature will drop from the normal range (38º–39ºC) to just under 38ºC.

Labour normally proceeds without complication, but urgent medical attention can be required if problems arise. To ensure the safety of the mother and her kittens, the cat should be watched throughout her labour until the kittens are born safely.

Once in labour, contractions ripple across the cat's body. The kittens will usually all be born within five hours, but times vary according to the individual cat and the size of the litter.

Cats normally give birth to four, five or six kittens, though litters of eight are not unusual and some are considerably larger – see box above.

Kittens can be born feet first or head first. Each kitten is enclosed in a sac and has an umbilical cord attached to

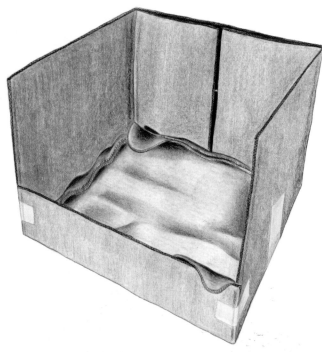

A strong cardboard box with some panels removed makes an ideal kittening box. Ensure that it is big enough for the cat to stretch out in and make sure there is a lip around the base so kittens cannot be easily pushed out.

Big families

The record for the most kittens in a single litter is held by a cat called Tarawood Antigone, owned by Valerie Gane from Church Westcote, Oxfordshire. On 7 August 1970 the four-year-old Burmese cat gave birth to 19 kittens by caesarean; 14 males and 1 female survived.

The record for the most kittens in a lifetime goes to a moggy from Texas called Dusty, who had given birth to 420 kittens by the time of her death in 1952.

his belly. The mother will wash the kitten to remove the sac and to stimulate breathing and circulation. She will then chew through the umbilical cord, leaving around 2 cm of cord on the kitten which will wither and fall away later.

It is normal for a cat to pass a placenta for each kitten and to eat these placentas. On rare occasions she may retain a placenta – this can cause health problems in the future. Let your vet know if you think that your cat hasn't passed all her placentas, but do not under any circumstances try to get the placenta out by pulling on the umbilical cord.

Once the labour is finished, remove the soiled kitchen towel from the delivery box, leaving just the clean, soft, dry bedding beneath. All kittens should take some milk from their mother within 12 hours.

The mother and kittens should be seen by a vet within 24 hours to make sure all is well and to check that all the kittens have been born. It is normal for the mother to have some bloody discharge for up to seven days after delivery. She should be seen by a vet if it continues for longer.

HELPING OUT

Mother cats rarely need help with labour and you should intervene only if it is absolutely necessary. Some of the more common problems include:

A kitten becoming stuck – if a kitten or a bubble (part of the birth sac) is partially visible but there is no progress for more than 10 minutes, your cat may need assistance. Take a clean, dampened cloth and use it to break the bubble. Then take hold of the kitten's head or feet. When a contraction comes along (seen as a ripple down the mother's body), firmly pull down on the kitten towards the mother cat's back feet. If this does not help, or if the mother cat cries loudly when you pull, then you should contact a vet immediately.

A kitten suffocating – if the mother does not remove the sac enclosing the kitten within a few minutes of delivery, the kitten will begin to suffocate. Use a clean, damp cloth to wash the kitten's face to remove the sac. Then take a warm, dry towel and rub the kitten to stimulate breathing and circulation. Tie the umbilical cord with cotton thread just less than 2 cm from the kitten's body and cut the cord with a disinfected pair of scissors.

Fluid on the lungs – if a kitten wheezes and has a blue tongue, liquid in his lungs may be obstructing his breathing. Hold your hand palm up and put the kitten in it with his head in between the forefinger and middle finger. Cover him with your other hand to hold him firmly in place and then swing with a smooth downward motion to try to loosen the fluid from the lungs. You may need to repeat this motion a number of times before the kitten's breathing is clear.

Exhaustion, collapse or miscarriage – if the mother appears exhausted, if there is a fresh (i.e. a bright red rather than deep red) bloody discharge for longer than 10 minutes, or if there are more than 20 minutes of intense contractions and no kittens are born, a vet should be called.

   If problems occur, your cat may need a caesarean section (a surgical operation to remove the kittens from the uterus). This is a serious operation and, although a cat usually recovers quickly, she may need help with caring for her litter at first.

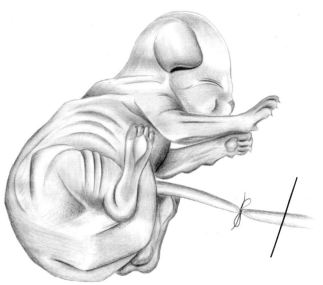

If the mother does not chew through the umbilical cord, you may have to help by tying the cord with cotton and cutting it yourself.

This cat is licking her new-born kitten clean while she continues labour.

RAISING KITTENS

Most mother cats know instinctively what to do to raise their kittens but there is still plenty of work for you to do just checking that everything is going well. As the kittens get older it will be your responsibility to make sure they are well fed, receive the right veterinary attention, become well socialized, and that they go to live in loving, responsible homes.

Feeding and growing

For the first few days after delivery the mother cat will spend all her time with her kittens – except when she eats or uses the litter tray. For the first two weeks, the kittens will spend 90 per cent of their time sleeping or eating. Every few hours, check that the kittens are warm and fed and that their mother is producing enough milk, but otherwise leave them alone. Do not intervene in feeding unless you think that there is a problem – see page 113.

The mother must be given as much high-energy kitten food as she wants while she is nursing so she can produce enough milk for her kittens. She must always have access to water. As well as feeding her kittens, she will also lick their genitals to encourage them to urinate and defecate.

At just over 2 weeks of age, the kittens' eyes will open and they will begin to explore in a haphazard and noisy way. At 3 weeks old they should become steady on their feet and begin playing.

After 4 weeks, the kittens will start to become interested in their mother's food and will stop suckling milk – this process is called weaning. The mother cat will by this time probably be very tired with producing and feeding so much milk, so to encourage kittens to wean you can soften dry kitten food in some watered-down milk formula and place the kittens near it so that their noses are close. In time they will automatically start eating.

Kittens should be fed on special kitten food until they are a year old but the mother can return to adult food after all the kittens are weaned as long as her weight is good.

Health and wellbeing

Kittens are given some antibodies in the first drink of their mother's milk, but after a few weeks these stop working and the kittens become vulnerable to diseases. Your vet should visit your home after the birth to ensure that mother and kittens are in good health and to advise about worming, flea treatment and vaccination. They should be treated for worms at around 6 weeks, and vaccinated at 8 and then 12 weeks old. They can be neutered from 16 weeks. Timings vary, so you should follow the advice of your vet.

It is important that between the ages of 4 and 12 weeks the kittens are properly socialized with normal household noises, people and other animals. These initial introductions to normal life – called being raised 'under foot' – help to create balanced, happy kittens. Kittens should remain with their mother and littermates until at least 8 or 9 weeks old, but many breeders will not home them until they have all had their booster vaccinations at 12 weeks.

Motherly devotion

In 1996 a mother cat called Scarlett amazed the world by repeatedly entering a burning building in Brooklyn to rescue her litter of kittens. Ignoring her horrendous burns, she returned to the building five times in all and became something of a celebrity for this exceptional display of motherly love.

Most mothers know instinctively how to raise kittens, but it is exhausting and the mother's health should be watched carefully.

These three 12-week-old kittens are completely independent and ready to leave their mother.

HELPING OUT

Mother cats rarely need help raising kittens, so you should intervene only if it is absolutely necessary. Some of the more common problems include:

Chilling – inside a house in a draught-free environment the mother's body heat will keep the kittens warm enough. The mother should leave the kittens only briefly to eat or go to the toilet. If she leaves them for longer periods they can rapidly become too cold. The kittens should be kept at about 30°C for the first few days, but this can be gradually reduced to about 22°C by the end of the fourth week. Large litters are better able to keep their heat and so will not need as much assistance if left alone.

Stress – an anxious mother may keep trying to move or hide her kittens. If she chooses to move them to a safe and accessible location, it is better to leave her where she is comfortable and try to avoid interfering. In some cases, though, particularly when dealing with cats that are not happy around humans, it is necessary to keep the mother enclosed in a room so that she cannot hide the kittens.

Hunger – if the kittens cry continuously or are not putting on weight, they may not be getting enough milk. If this is happening, or if there are more than five kittens in the litter, the mother's milk will need to be supplemented with a warmed kitten-feed formula – consult your vet before you embark on this. If the kittens are getting some milk from their mother, you will need

to feed less than the full amount recommended on the formula. If the kittens are not getting any milk, feed them the full recommended amount divided into regular small meals throughout each 24-hour period.

Kittens less than 2 weeks old must be fed every 2.5 hours – ten times in every 24 hours. Kittens between 2 and 4 weeks of age need to be fed every 3.5 hours (seven times every 24 hours. Weaning (changing on to solid food) should begin at around 4 weeks, at which point kittens should be fed every 5 hours in about five separate feeds. It is vital that kittens are neither over- nor under-fed.

Illness – if the kittens cry continuously, even after they appear to have eaten, they may be sick. Call a vet to have the mother and kittens checked.

Weak, abandoned or undernourished kittens may need to be hand-fed with formula.

Milk fever – mother cats, especially those with large litters, may start to suffer from a lack of calcium because of the stresses of producing so much milk. This usually occurs when the kittens are between 3 and 5 weeks old. Spasms, panting and locked legs are signs that a mother has milk fever. A vet should be called as soon as signs are noticed as this condition develops rapidly and can be fatal in less than an hour.

Orphans – on rare occasions, a mother cat may refuse to take care of her kittens or may die during labour. In these circumstances the kittens will need to be cared for entirely by you. This will include:
- Complete milk-formula feeding for the first four weeks, as described above.
- A carefully maintained room temperature – see above.
- Stimulation of the kittens' genital area to make them urinate and defecate – you must do this for the first two weeks by taking a moist cloth and massaging the area. Without this assistance, kittens may become constipated.

Kittens will struggle to survive without their mother and hand-rearing is not always successful, so you must be prepared for some or all of the kittens to die despite your best efforts.

A changing relationship

There may come a point, usually around weaning time, when a mother cat will start to act differently towards her kittens, such as lashing out or growling at them when they approach her. Although it is awful to see, this is a perfectly normal part of the distancing process through which a mother forces her kittens to become independent. If you think that the kittens are in serious danger, you can separate the mother and kittens once they are fully weaned, though this is not normally necessary.

Chapter 7

SHOWING YOUR CAT

Some cat enthusiasts like to 'show' their cats. Showing is aimed at pedigree cats, but there are often classes within shows that are open to non-pedigrees as well.

The aim of shows is to find the best example of a breed or, in the case of non-pedigrees, the best health and temperament. Cats are judged against a list of attributes for each breed – called the breed standard – and the closer to 'perfection' they come, the higher they will score in the results. There are a number of governing bodies that run cat shows, each one offering different titles. The humblest titles are available at local shows, with the most prized being awarded to the winners of national and international shows.

Prizes may include titles, certificates or rosettes. The majority of entrants show for the prestige of winning or simply for fun. Cash prizes are sometimes given, but this is not a hobby to enter into if you plan to make money – the costs far outweigh the financial rewards.

Research, rules and registration

It is important to do your research carefully before you start showing as a hobby.

BREEDS

If you haven't got a cat yet, look at the different breeds. Don't forget that some available breeds are not recognized by governing bodies and so cannot be shown. For example, certain breeds with a genetic deformity as part of their breed characteristic or breeds that have been developed very recently may be excluded. For details of cat breeds, see pages 16–21.

Choose your breed and start by contacting the breed club in your area. The members of the breed club will be able to give you advice about showing, where to get good-quality kittens, and about the standards for the breed (e.g. what a judge will be looking for in the show ring).

Some breed clubs have their own websites, but all registered clubs will be listed by the various governing bodies. The three key governing bodies in the UK are the Governing Council of the Cat Fancy (GCCF), Felis Britannica (FB – part of the international Fédération Internationale Féline (FIFe)), and The International Cat Association (TICA). For contact details, see page 126. Each has its own rules and regulations which must be strictly followed to avoid disqualification.

PREPARATION

Begin by purchasing a show-quality neutered kitten. These kittens are not registered for breeding but can be shown in neutered classes at shows. A reputable breeder will be able to tell you which kittens from their litter are of show quality, but if you know anyone who is experienced with the breed, take them along too. Don't forget to look for a relaxed and friendly kitten, just as you would when choosing any cat, as showing can be quite traumatic for less sociable cats and it will only work if you both enjoy it.

Listings of forthcoming regional shows can be found through your breed club contacts, via one of the governing bodies or on the internet. For your first show, choose one that is at least three months away and that is taking place close to your home so you don't need to take your kitten too far.

Once you know which show you want to attend, read the general rules of the governing body that runs the show to make sure that your cat qualifies. To enter the show you will need to request a show schedule and entry form from the show manager – details will be found with the show listing.

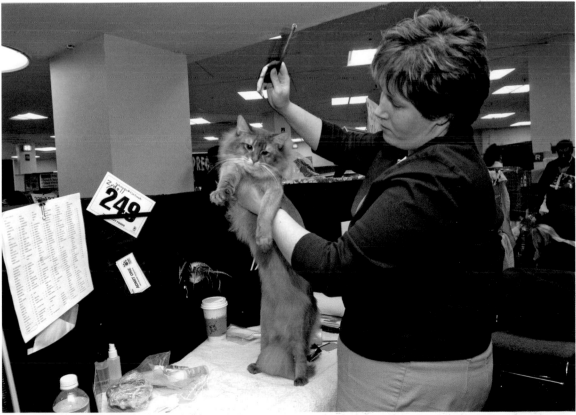

Some last-minute preparations before the show.

MAKING YOUR APPLICATION

When the schedule and entry form arrive, read the schedule carefully as it will contain extra show and club rules, the list of classes for the show and details for entrants, such as expected arrival time and equipment you must bring. Classes are arranged differently depending on the type of show you are attending, but often include divisions by breed, age, colour, sex and whether the cat is neutered or not. You will need to read through the classes carefully and decide which ones your cat will enter.

The entry form includes questions about:
* The classes you are entering.
* The registered owners of the cat (you and any joint owners).
* The cat being shown (you will need his registration papers if he is a pedigree).

Don't forget to sign the declaration and include a cheque for your entry fees before sending the application to the show manager. Before the show, you will receive all your paperwork outlining which classes you have entered and all your details. Double-check that all the information is correct as any mistakes may mean disqualification later.

At some shows, onlookers can watch the judging and listen to judges' comments.

VACCINATIONS, HEALTH AND CLEANING

There is an increased risk of diseases being transferred at shows, so there are strict rules about the health of cats that are entered. All cats must be:
* Up to date with their vaccinations.
* Free from parasites (fleas, ear mites and ticks – see pages 84, 88 and 92–93).
* In good health (no sneezing, runny eyes or skin problems). For advice on health, see Chapter 4.

Before the show you should also make sure that your cat's ears and eyes are clean, and that his claws are trimmed (see pages 68–69).

EQUIPMENT

Check the schedule and make sure you bring the required equipment. It usually includes:
* A good-quality cat carrier (see page 73).
* A couple of clean, plain, white blankets.
* White bowls for food and water.
* A white litter tray.
* White tape or elastic to secure your cat's tally (registration number) around his neck.
* Disinfectant wipes for the show pen.

Note that equipment is required to be white. This is so that no competitor's equipment will have any distinguishing features that might allow the judge to identify the breeder of a particular cat.

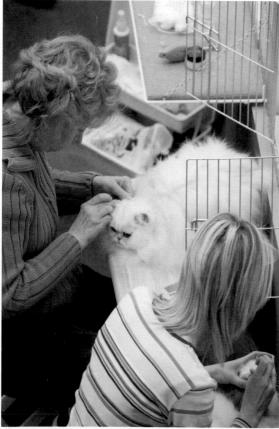

Clean eyes and ears are vital for a show cat.

On the day

Shows usually last for one day only. Check your schedule again to make sure you know when to get there and that you have everything you need.

When you arrive, go to 'Vetting-in'. Here a vet will look over your vaccination card and check your cat to make sure he is in good health. If all is fine, the vet will sign your vetting-in card to say that your cat is free to participate in the show.

From vetting-in you can go to your allotted pen. Pens are numbered and arranged in rows of classes or breeds. Put your cat in his pen, make sure he is comfortable and give him a little food and some water. When it is time for the judging, you will have to leave your cat in his pen. Make sure that you remove his food bowl and that both he and his pen (including the white blanket and litter tray) are clean and tidy.

After the judging, you will be allowed back to see your cat and to check the results board to see if he has been placed. Depending on the show, winning cats may be required to wait to be judged in further rounds, but if your cat hasn't won and if he has no other classes, you can both go home and relax.

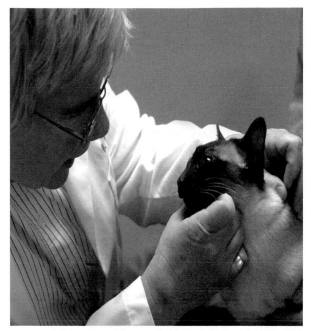

Before being able to enter classes at a show, all cats need to be passed at 'vetting-in'.

At most smaller shows in the UK, judges make their way round the pens.

THE BEST OF THE BEST

National Championship Shows

There are three levels of title your cat can win at national Championship Shows.

At these shows, cats are inspected by judges moving from pen to pen, and begin by winning Challenge Certificates (for entire cats) or Premier Certificates (for neutered cats). Once a cat has won three certificates, awarded by three different judges, he can claim the title:
Champion or **Premier**

A Champion or Premier cat can enter special Grand Classes at Championship Shows to win Grand Certificates. Again, he needs to be awarded three certificates, awarded by three different judges, to claim the title:
Grand Champion or **Grand Premier**

Once a Grand Champion or Grand Premier, your cat can enter the Imperial Grand Class at Championship Shows. In this class he needs five certificates, from five different judges, before claiming the title:
Imperial Grand Champion or
Imperial Grand Premier

GCCF Supreme Cat Show

The largest, most popular cat show in the UK is the annual Governing Council of the Cat Fancy (GCCF) Supreme Cat Show.

At this event, held in late November, cats are judged in show rings, where onlookers can listen to the judges' comments as they look at each cat in the class. It is therefore a great show for newcomers to visit before embarking on showing their cat, as you can learn a great deal from watching what goes on and listening to what the judges have to say.

Cats are divided into three classes:

1. Imperial Grand Champion, Grand Champion, Imperial Grand Premier and Grand Premier title holders.
2. Champion and Premier title holders.
3. Cats with no previous title.

Cats in the Imperial and Grand classes may be awarded a UK Certificate. Two of these certificates from two different judges allow the winner to claim the title:
UK Imperial Grand Champion or
UK Imperial Grand Premier

Cats in all classes at the GCCF Supreme Cat Show are eligible to win **Best of Variety** for the year as **Supreme Adult** or **Supreme Neuter** or **Supreme Kitten**

Money prizes are rare; most owners compete for the prestige of titles.

Cat shows

The very first cat show on record took place in Winchester in 1598, but was little more than a side show at the St Giles' Fair. One of the prizes awarded was for the best mouser. The first cat show in the grand form that we know today was held in London's Crystal Palace in 1871.

Chapter 8

YOUR CAT AND THE LAW

Owning any animal, whether domestic or agricultural, brings with it certain responsibilities both towards the animal itself and towards other people who may come into contact with your animal. There are therefore several laws that affect your cat and your responsibilities as an owner – and also that protect your rights.

Your responsibilities

These laws relate to your responsibilities as an owner.

Animal Welfare Act 2006: aims to promote the welfare of all animals and to prevent cruelty. It says that animals cannot be purchased by anyone under the age of 16 and it requires that all cat owners (or people with responsibilities for cats, such as cattery owners) give their cats:

- Protection from injury, disease, suffering and pain.
- The opportunity to carry out natural behaviour.
- A proper place to live.
- A suitable diet.

Under this law, failure to do these things can be considered cruelty and may result in a fine of up to £20,000, imprisonment (for severe cases) and a ban on owning animals.

Environmental Protection Act 1990: your local Environmental Health Department is able to intervene when it feels that a property presents a nuisance or health hazard because there are too many cats being kept there. If you keep more cats than is considered appropriate for a normal domestic household, your Local Authority may require that you apply for a change of use for your property so that it is registered as a cattery.

Animal Act 1971: this law recognizes that cats are less likely than many other animals to cause damage to property or to injure people and so there is no requirement to keep your cat on your own land. However, you do have a general duty to ensure that your cat does not cause damage or injury.

Your rights

Cats are considered to be legal property. The following laws relate to your rights as a cat owner:

Criminal Damage Act 1971: this law prohibits the killing or injuring of another person's cat.

Theft Act 1968: this law prohibits the stealing of a cat. Any cat found straying is still considered the legal property of the original owner.

Delinquent cats . . .

It is very rare for a cat to cause any sort of serious damage to other people or their property, but not unheard of. Along with the usual stories of ripped curtains or sofas, cats have been known to cause far more serious problems, such as the two Japanese kittens who, in 2005, set their house on fire by urinating in the fax machine; and Bat, the ginger tom from Kent, whose owner had to collect his post from the sorting centre after postmen got fed up with being attacked by the cat and refused to deliver any more mail.

Chapter 9

FANTASTIC CATS

If you are already a cat owner, you will be well aware that they are amazing creatures with a talent for getting into everything. It's no surprise then that they have not only managed to get into the history books, but have also become the subject of legends, wise sayings and superstitions. Here are just a few of the ways in which cats, both real and fictional, have made an impression on the world.

THE DOWNFALL OF EGYPT

Legend says that the might of the Egyptian army was crushed by the Persian King Cambyses at the battle of Pelusium in 525 BC when he adopted the very strange tactic of having his soldiers carry cats in front of them into battle. The Egyptians were so distraught by the thought of hurting the animals, which they revered as gods, that they were easily subdued and Cambyses succeeded in storming Pelusium. After the battle, Cambyses himself taunted the Egyptians by riding through the city with a cage of cats in front of him on his horse and hurling them at his defeated foes.

Was it really the Ancient Egyptians' reverence for the cat that toppled their mighty empire?

PIGEON ON THE MENU

During the short reign of Richard III, Sir Henry Wyatt (1460–1537) was imprisoned in the Tower of London because of his support for Henry Tudor's claim to the throne. Barely fed and badly treated, he would almost certainly have perished if it hadn't been for the actions of a certain cat.

Facing starvation, one day Sir Henry was visited in his cell by a cat and the two became friends. This new companion no doubt raised Sir Henry's spirits, but also had the rather useful habit of bringing along a pigeon as a present, which Sir Henry duly dined on. In this way Wyatt survived two years of imprisonment, being released only on the death of Richard and the accession of Henry VII in 1485.

The cat's kindness is remembered on a stone memorial in the church of St Mary the Virgin and All Saints in Maidstone, Kent: 'To the memory of Sir Henry Wiat [Wyatt], of Alington Castle . . . who was imprisoned and tortured in the Tower, in the reign of King Richard the third, kept in the dungeon, where fed and preserved by a cat.'

A VERY FINE CAT INDEED

Samuel Johnson (1709–84), essayist and compiler of the first English dictionary, had an accomplice during his years of research and writing: his cat Hodge. Johnson's biographer, James Boswell, recounts that when he remarked that Hodge was a fine cat, Johnson replied that he had had better cats. However, on seeing that Hodge was wounded by this flippant remark, he added the now famous line, 'But he is a very fine cat, a very fine cat indeed.' Hodge needn't have worried about being under-appreciated, as this little remark has made him something of a celebrity and a bronze statue of him sitting on a dictionary with an oyster at his feet (his favourite food) stands outside Johnson's house in London's Gough Square as a permanent reminder of this very fine companion.

IMPECCABLE BEHAVIOUR

The only cat to have won the Dickin Medal for outstanding bravery in war – the animal equivalent of the Victoria Cross – was Simon, a Hong Kong-born cat who was adopted as a rat-catcher by the crew of HMS *Amethyst* during the Second World War. In 1949 the ship was sent to China and came under attack from Communist batteries on the shore of the Yangtze river. For two months this drastic situation continued in deadlock. Despite being seriously wounded by shrapnel, Simon continued to catch rats aboard the ship and to keep up the morale of injured seamen.

On the crew's eventual escape to Hong Kong, news of the ship's ordeal and Simon's dedication to his duties spread, and it was decided that he should receive the Dickin Medal. It was to be presented to him in the UK on 11 December 1949, but sadly Simon fell ill in quarantine and died just a few days before, on 28 November.

Simon lies at the PDSA animal cemetery in Ilford, his grave marked with the words 'In memory of Simon, served in HMS *Amethyst*, May 1948–September 1949. Awarded the Dickin Medal August 1949. Died 28th November 1949. Throughout the Yangtze incident his behaviour was of the highest order'. He remains the only cat ever to have won the Dickin Medal.

A LUCKY GUEST

If you book a table for 13 people at London's famous Savoy Grill, your party will be joined by an uninvited guest: a metre high statue of a black cat called Kaspar.

The tradition started in 1898 after an unlucky South African guest named Woolf Joel held a dinner party attended by only 13 people. All his guests knew the superstition about a terrible fate befalling the first person to rise from a dinner table of 13, but Woolf Joel

Simon was a cat with sea legs and a brave heart. A feline admirer is brought to see his award.

took no notice of such silly beliefs and exited first after dinner, unconcerned about his future. On his return to South Africa shortly afterwards, however, he was tragically shot dead.

Since then, the Savoy hasn't allowed a dinner party of 13 to sit without providing an extra guest to make the number up to 14. At first this was a member of staff, but in the 1920s Kaspar was commissioned by the hotel and created by artist Basil Ionides. He has been the fourteenth member of groups ever since.

BORN TO BE WILD

Cats are not usually keen on travel, but there are some rather odd exceptions and Rastus was one of those. Rastus belonged to New Zealand biker Max Corkhill and, rather than running at the sound of a bike engine, Rastus would grab his specially made goggles and helmet and jump on board for a spin. The two became famous in their local town, New Plymouth in the Taranaki region of North Island. People would gawp in astonishment as the biker and his helmet-clad cat, perched on top of the petrol tank, whizzed by. Their celebrity status meant Max was able to raise money by selling Max and Rastus goods; much of the profit was donated to animal welfare charities.

Sadly, on 20 January 1998, the pair and another pillion passenger were killed in a head-on collision with a car. The driver of the other vehicle went to prison for dangerous driving and Max and Rastus were cremated together in a ceremony attended by more than 1,000 bikers.

Cat proverbs

1. When the cat's away, the mice will play. – *English*
2. A cat bitten once by a snake dreads even rope. – *Arabian*
3. A cat has nine lives. For three he plays, for three he strays, and for the last three he stays. – *English*
4. A cat may look at a king. – *English*
5. The cat's a saint when there are no mice about. – *Japanese*
6. I gave an order to a cat, and the cat gave it to its tail. – *Chinese*
7. Those who dislike cats will be carried to the cemetery in the rain. – *Dutch*
8. When rats infest the Palace a lame cat is better than the swiftest horse. – *Chinese*
9. Happy is the home with at least one cat. – *Italian*
10. Wherever the mice laugh at the cat, there you will find a hole. – *Portuguese*

CARTOON CATS

Fantastic cats

Felix the Cat was the original cartoon cat. Created by Otto Messner in the early 1920s, the black-and-white cat first appeared in American silent animated films and as a comic strip. Since then he has starred in numerous film, cartoon, song and newspaper roles and is still going strong today in various forms.

Tom and Jerry made their first screen appearance in the 1940 cartoon *Puss Gets the Boot*, and subsequently were the stars of well over 100 animated short films made by William Hanna and Joseph Barbera. From the 1960s until the 1990s they appeared in their own TV series, and several Tom and Jerry films have been made. Tom, the determined cat, and his clever nemesis, Jerry the mouse, set about trying to outdo each other in every story, usually culminating in Tom being unceremoniously booted out of the house. New short films are still being made, and the pair have seven times won Academy Awards – the greatest number of awards ever achieved by an animated series.

Si and Am, the two memorable Siamese cats from the animated Disney feature film *Lady and the Tramp* (1955), gave their breed a bad name with their nonchalant antics, but won fans around the world while they were at it – just like the real thing.

For over sixty years cartoon characters Tom and Jerry have fought like cat and . . . mouse.

'Hello Kitty' is a small, white, unimposing kitten with a very big bank balance. The popular Japanese character was created by the Sanrio company in 1974, first depicted on a small plastic purse, and has since appeared on a vast range of merchandise, from stationery to cars. She has also featured in a TV series and a number of video games. Her sales are around $1 billion a year.

Sylvester the Cat was one of the main characters of the animated series *Looney Tunes*, made in the USA from 1945 until 1966. Sylvester's nemesis was a tiny yellow canary called Tweety Pie. Whilst easily able to defend himself from sly Sylvester, Tweety Pie could also rely on Granny to shoo the poor cat away. Sufferin' succotash!

Top Cat was the hero of a popular American TV series of that name. TC, as he was known to his mates, was the leader of a band of alley cats who spent their time trying to avoid Officer Dibble, who was determined to throw them out of their alley. The 30 episodes, made by Hanna–Barbera, ran between 1961 and 1962.

Garfield, the overweight ginger tom with the biting wit, was created by Jim Davis in 1978 as a daily comic strip. More than thirty years later, he is still going strong, and is now the world's most widely syndicated comic strip – in 2007 he was appearing in 2,580 newspapers and journals around the globe. He has also starred in television specials and in two films. Garfield hates Mondays, loves lasagne and enjoys tormenting his dog companion, Odie.

Bagpuss, created for the BBC by Peter Firmin and Oliver Postgate and brought to life through stop motion animation, oversaw a little girl called Emily's shop full of old, lost and abandoned toys and objects. Only 13 episodes were ever made, but the baggy old cloth cat has remained a firm favourite with later generations of British children.

Doraemon, a Japanese animated (*anime*) robotic cat, has been spreading moral messages – such as treating elders with respect, looking after the environment and helping homeless animals – since 1961. He first appeared in children's magazines, and later in his own TV show. However, the character shot to worldwide fame in 2008 when he was made Japan's *anime* ambassador by the country's foreign ministry, with the task of encouraging interest in Japanese culture worldwide.

Jess, the black-and-white cat belonging to Postman Pat, first appeared on the BBC in 1981. Drawn by John Cunliffe, Jess has since accompanied Pat on numerous postal deliveries and has been seen on TV screens across the world, from Australia to Iran. In 2008 the pair launched a new series called *Postman Pat Special Delivery Service*, where old Jess gets to ride in a whole array of vehicles, from helicopters to motorbike side-cars.

A GORILLA'S CAT

In 1984, in Woodside, California, a gorilla called Koko, who had been trained to use American Sign Language, asked her keeper, Dr Francine Patterson, for a cat. From a litter of abandoned kittens, after carefully examining them all, Koko chose a grey, tailless, male Manx cat, and named him All Ball. Koko tended the kitten, letting him ride on her back and using sign language to ask him to play 'tickle' – Koko's favourite game. She even signed to her keepers, 'Koko love All Ball'.

In December 1984, while still only a few months old, All Ball escaped from the gorilla's cage and was hit by a car. Upon learning from her keepers that All Ball was dead, Koko, who had a vocabulary of over 500 words, signed 'Cry. Sleep cat.' All Ball was followed by two other adopted kittens – Lipstick and Smoky – both of whom were also tailless Manx cats chosen by Koko herself.

TINY CATS

A tabby named Mr Peebles was officially recognized as the world's smallest living cat by the *Guinness Book of Records* in 2004. When he was rescued from a farm in Illinois in 2002 by the visiting vet, he had ear mites, roundworms, a respiratory infection, was underweight and under constant threat both from his bigger siblings and from the local horned owl population.

Despite being fed four times a day, Mr Peebles weighs only 1.4 kg and measures a mere 15.25 cm in height. His size is the result of a genetic defect that limits growth.

Subsequently the *Guinness Book of Records* recognized Itse-Bitse, who stands at 9.52 cm high and 38.1 cm long as the smallest living cat. She herself is now being challenged for the title by Tinker Toy, a male blue point Himalayan Persian cat. like Mr Peebles living in Illinois, who is said to be just 7 cm tall and 19 cm long.

FREYA'S CATS

The warrior and fertility goddess Freya was worshipped by the Norsemen for her beauty. People would pray to her for help in love and in childbirth, in preparing for war, and to ask for a good harvest. Her many talents reflect her very high status among the Norse gods and, as befits such a high-ranking deity, she had not one but two modes of transport. Thor, the god of thunder, had a chariot pulled by goats, and even the chief god Odin himself had only a horse, but Freya had both a golden boar and a golden chariot, which was pulled across the sky by two Norwegian Forest cats given to her by Thor.

All cats were sacred to Freya, and farmers would leave out precious milk for them, to ensure that she blessed their harvest. When a bride had good weather on her wedding day, people would remark, 'She has fed the cat well', meaning that she had kept the goddess of love on her side. For an actual cat to appear at the wedding was a sure sign of a very happy marriage.

Cat superstitions

1. A black cat crossing your path is said to be good luck in the UK but bad luck in the USA.
2. If a cat washes his ears and paws in the parlour, you will have visitors.
3. If a cat leaves the house of someone who is unwell, then death is near.
4. If a young, unmarried woman steps on a cat's tail, she will be married in less than a year.
5. In Italy it is said that anyone who hears a cat sneeze will receive good luck.
6. If the first thing you see in the morning is two cats playing, then the rest of your day will be wasted.
7. If you have a stye on your eye, stroke the tail of a black cat against it and you will be cured.
8. In France it is considered bad luck to try to cross a stream carrying a cat.
9. If a cat rushes about wildly, expect a strong wind.
10. In the Netherlands any private family discussions must be held out of earshot of the family cat, as he will only spread the gossip around town.

MUEZZA AND MOHAMMED

Islam insists that all animals are treated with respect. Cats are particularly revered because Mohammed himself had a cat called Muezza, whom he loved very much. One famous story tells that once, as Mohammed was called to prayer, he found Muezza sleeping on the sleeve of his robe. Instead of waking the cat, he cut off the sleeve and put on what was left of his robe, leaving the cat to sleep undisturbed. The Prophet often gave sermons with little Muezza on his lap, and once took his ablution from a bowl of water that a cat had just been drinking.

Mohammed's deep respect for these little creatures began when he was saved by a cat from a snake which had curled up in his shoe. It is often said that the 'M' that appears on a tabby cat's forehead is a mark from Mohammed himself.

FAIRY CATS OF THE HIGHLANDS

A legend of the Scottish Highlands told of a clan of huge, black fairy cats called the Cath Sith, whose king, Big Ears, could be summoned forth to answer questions by spitting and roasting a live cat over a fire (a form of divination known as *taghgairm*). The real Cath Sith may actually have been a large, black wild cat called the Kellas cat, which was finally rediscovered in 1984 after a gamekeeper shot and killed one. Kellas cats are around 63 cm long, their DNA suggesting that they were originally a mix of European wild cat and domestic cats. No doubt due to the practice of roasting them alive, these Kellas cats had become extremely wary of humans, which explains why their existence passed into myth. Fortunately for the Kellas cat, *taghgairm* is no longer practised in the Highlands.

PECULIAR CAT NAMES

It was the poet T. S. Eliot who claimed in *Old Possum's Book of Practical Cats* that a cat must have at least three names – one ordinary, one peculiar and dignified, and one that only he knows. Over the years, many owners have done their best with peculiar and dignified names, as the following demonstrate:

Misty Malarky Ying Yang, the Siamese cat of former US President Jimmy Carter.

Blatherskite and **Sour Mash**, two of the many cats that belonged to the writer Mark Twain.

Goody Two Eyes, who belonged to Ella Wheeler Wilcox (1850–1919), the American poet and author who wrote the line 'Laugh, and the world laughs with you; Weep, and you weep alone.'

Bing Clawsby, owned by Michael Feinstein, the American singer and pianist.

Chairman Meow belongs to comedian David Baddiel. His comedy partner, Frank Skinner, is rumoured to hate the cat and once put him in Room 101.

Gladstone was the large Persian cat who belonged to the nurse Florence Nightingale and was named after William Gladstone, four times prime minister in the nineteenth century.

George Pushdragon and **Jellylorum** are among the many noted feline companions of the poet T. S. Eliot. Jellylorum even had her own starring role in *Old Possum's Book of Practical Cats*, in the poem 'The Naming of Cats'.

Le Docteur belonged to Alexandre Dumas (1824–95), author of *The Three Musketeers*.

Poo Jones was owned by actress Vivien Leigh, who won an Academy Award for the role of Scarlett O'Hara in the film *Gone with the Wind*.

And finally . . . **The Most Noble, the Archduke Rumpelstiltzchen, Marcus Macbum, Earl Tomlefnagne, Baron Raticide, Waowhler and Scratch** . . . or Rumpel for short. This magnificently named animal's owner, Poet Laureate Robert Southey (1774–1843), wrote upon the cat's death, 'I believe we are each and all, servants included, more sorry for his loss, or, rather, more affected by it, than any of us would like to confess.'

The amazing cheetah

Everybody knows that the world's fastest land animal – the cheetah – is a cat. It can run at over 60mph. But did you also know that while a cheetah cannot roar, it purrs instead.

THE CAT ADAPTS

Cats are nature's survivors, and have made some fantastic adaptations in order to spread across the entire world. The giant Amur or Siberian tiger grows to over 3 metres long and, because of its extremely thick winter coat, survives Russian winters that regularly hit temperatures as low as -40°C.

Meanwhile, the North African desert sandcat has adapted to the endless drought by drinking no water at all, but getting the liquid it needs only from the food that it can catch. The fishing cat, found in the rivers and swamps of some parts of Asia, has partially webbed paws so he can swim, dive and catch fish in his watery habitat.

THE BECKONING CAT

A common talisman used throughout Japan to bring luck is that of the *maneki-neko* or beckoning cat. According to the often-told story, the Gotokuji Temple cat, Tama, repaid the poverty-stricken priest who cared for him by bringing prosperity to the temple. One day, as a storm raged, Tama beckoned to a passing samurai, Ii Naotaka. As the samurai approached, lightning struck the spot where he had been standing – the little cat had saved his life. In return, Ii Naotaka became a patron of the Gotokuji Temple and it has been in his family ever since.

To this day, little ceramic *maneki-neko* are used as a symbol of fortune and good luck by business proprietors all over Japan. The beckoning cats can often be seen waving through shop windows at passers-by, inviting them to come in.

AN UNFORTUNATE SHIPMATE

Ernest Shackleton's miraculous polar survival story is well known. Having left London in August 1914 aiming to trek from sea to sea across Antarctica, his ship, *Endurance*, became stuck in the polar ice. His crew was forced into a two-year fight for survival while Shackleton himself made a perilous 800-mile journey to a whaling station and returned to rescue his men in August 1916.

What is less well-known is that, before setting off on his rescue mission, Shackleton ordered that all the sledge dogs and the ship's cat, Mrs Chippy, be shot. Mrs Chippy belonged to the ship's carpenter, Harry McNeish, who clashed bitterly with Shackleton over the incident. Nevertheless, after sad farewells from the crew and a last meal of sardines, the cat was allowed to settle down and was then shot.

Relations between Shackleton and McNeish didn't improve on their return to England. Despite his courage and determination throughout the ordeal, and despite building the boats that eventually helped save their lives, McNeish was denied the Polar Medal. Finally, in 2004, a bronze statue of Mrs Chippy was placed on McNeish's grave, in belated recognition of his efforts on the voyage and the sacrifices he made.

Cherie Blair with Humphrey, the subject of much controversy: did he jump or was he pushed?

UNSINKABLE SAM

A cat well known for his nine lives was Unsinkable Sam, a ship's cat who during the Second World War survived the sinking of three ships.

Originally called Oscar, he was a German ship's cat aboard the ill-fated battleship *Bismarck*, torpedoed in 1941. Only 116 of the 2,200 men on board survived. Oscar was then adopted by the Royal Navy ship that rescued him – the British destroyer HMS *Cossack*. Unfortunately, the *Cossack* was itself sunk in October 1941, at a cost of 159 lives. It was at this point that Oscar became known as Unsinkable Sam. He was transferred to HMS *Ark Royal* to continue active service, but soon after, this ship too was torpedoed and sunk, though only one crew member was killed. The cat again was unharmed.

Sam was finally retired to an old sailors' home, where he lived peacefully until his death in 1955. A portrait of him hangs in the National Maritime Museum in Greenwich, but recently doubt has been cast on his incredible story. Could a cat really have survived where so many died? Could it be that Sam was just war propaganda – a story to keep up morale? We may never know for sure.

THE CAT AT NUMBER 10

Humphrey the cat went from being an ordinary stray to a cat in the employment of the British government. He arrived in 1988, aged about one, and went on to give many years of service at 10 Downing Street. He was said to be a favourite of Margaret Thatcher, who was impressed that, at a measly £100 a year, Humphrey cost a lot less than getting in the exterminator. He went on to serve during John Major's tenure and was staunchly defended by the PM when it was reported that he had savagely eaten a nest of robin chicks.

Like many celebrities, Humphrey went out in a blaze of publicity. The Blairs moved into Number 10 in 1997 and within weeks it was announced that Humphrey was to be unceremoniously booted out. In the ensuing media storm it was rumoured that Cherie Blair had it in for poor Humphrey, but Downing Street quickly claimed that it was all untrue – Humphrey would remain in his home. A press shoot of Cherie cuddling Humphrey was hastily organized, but it was later admitted that the cat was sedated for the photograph.

Despite the protestations, Humphrey's days were indeed numbered and with the excuse that he needed proper care for his kidney disease, he was retired to a home in suburbia. If the Blairs hoped that this would be the end of the affair, they were to be disappointed. Humphrey remained a source of much interest and speculation – including questions in the House of Commons and allegations that Cherie had ordered his murder – and he continued to attract column inches right up until his death in 2006.

Fantastic cats

AN INSPIRATION . . .

Cats have, of course, appeared in art and literature throughout history, but Selima, who belonged to the fourth Earl of Orford, Horace Walpole, was notable in inspiring both an ode and a painting, and all through the manner of her death.

While trying to reach some goldfish kept in a large Chinese vase, Selima slipped, fell in and, unable to extract herself, drowned. Devastated by her death, the Earl asked his poet friend Thomas Gray to write an epitaph for his beloved cat. Gray went on to write a full ode entitled 'Ode on the Death of a Favourite Cat, Drowned in a Tub of Gold Fishes'. Then in 1776 Selima inspired even more artistic endeavours when artist Stephen Elmer painted a scene showing her hovering over the edge of a vase with a copy of Gray's ode sitting nearby. The painting was entitled *Horace Walpole's Favourite Cat*.

Delighted by the tributes to Selima, Walpole had the first stanza of the ode engraved on the fatal vase.

COPY CAT

The first cloned pet was CC, or Copy Cat, who is genetically identical to Rainbow, a tortie-and-white shorthaired cat. CC was the result of a research project, carried out at the College of Veterinary Medicine, Texas A & M University, aimed at cloning a dog called Missy. Although 87 embryos were produced, only CC went to full term.

In 2006 CC had her own kittens and, according to Dr Duane Kraemer, who now owns the cat, the whole family is healthy and normal.

USEFUL CONTACTS

AllergyUK

A charity that offers advice to allergy sufferers and recommends products to help ease symptoms.
Tel. 01322 619898
Email info@allergyuk.org
Web www.allergyuk.org

Association of Pet Behaviour Counsellors

An international network of pet behaviour counsellors who deal with a number of different species and offer advice on welfare.
Tel. 01386 751151
Email info@apbc.org.uk
Web www.apbc.org.uk

Association of Private Pet Cemeteries and Crematoria

This membership organization for pet cemeteries and crematoria promotes a code of practice for its members.
Tel. 01252 844478
Email contact@appcc.org.uk
Web www.appcc.org.uk

Battersea Dogs & Cats Home

This London-based charity rehomes cats and dogs and provides a lost and found service to reunite people with their pets. They also run a pet behaviour advice line for the general public.
Tel. 020 7622 3626
Web www.battersea.org.uk
Lost Dogs & Cats Line 0901 477 8477
Behaviour Advice Line 0905 020 0222

Blue Cross

Blue Cross is a charity aimed at all pets and horses. As well as rehoming animals, they also provide bereavement support for owners who have lost their pets.
Tel. 01993 822651
Email info@bluecross.org.uk
Web www.bluecross.org.uk

Blue Cross Pet Bereavement Support

Tel. 0800 096 6606
Email pbssmail@bluecross.org.uk

Cats Protection

The UK's largest cat welfare charity primarily rehomes and neuters cats, and is a useful source of information and advice. They also run a Diabetic Cat Register to help support owners with diabetic cats. The charity has a National Cat Adoption Centre in Sussex and a network of smaller branches and adoption centres across the UK.
Helpline 08702 099 099 (national rate)
Email cp@cats.org.uk
Web www.cats.org.uk

Department for Environment, Food and Rural Affairs (Defra)

Defra is a government department that offers information about animal welfare laws and the rules involving the transportation of animals in and out of the UK.
Tel. 08459 33 55 77
Email helpline@defra.gsi.gov.uk
Web www.defra.gov.uk

Feline Advisory Bureau (FAB)

This charity promotes the health and welfare of cats by improving feline knowledge.
Tel. 0870 742 2278
Email information@fabcats.org
Web www.fabcats.org

Felis Britannica (FB)

This organization is the representative for a federation of cat clubs in the UK which are part of the international body, Fédération Internationale Féline (FIFe).
Tel. 023 8046 3800
Email secretary@felisbritannica.co.uk
Web www.felisbritannica.co.uk

Governing Council of the Cat Fancy (GCCF)

The GCCF is a UK governing body for pedigree breeding and showing.
Tel. 01278 427575
Email info@gccfcats.org
Web www.gccfcats.org

National Association of Registered Petsitters (NARP)

This organization sets standards for pet- and house-sitting services and holds a register of UK companies offering these services. You must subscribe to receive the register, but you are able to see how many sitters there are in your area before paying the fee.
Tel. 08452 308544
Web www.dogsit.com

PDSA

This charity provides veterinary care for animals owned by people in need. You must live in the catchment area of one of their veterinary centres and must be entitled to assistance under their eligibility rules.
Tel. 01952 290999
Web www.pdsa.org.uk

Pet Sitter Swap

This small organization helps to put pet owners who live in the same area in touch with each other so they can swap pet-sitting services and essentially get a pet-sitter for free. Make sure you are completely happy with the person you intend to swap with before you give them access to your home.
Web www.petsitterswap.com

RSPCA

The RSPCA is primarily responsible for upholding animal welfare laws. They work with both companion and wild animals and they do some rehoming.
Advice Line 0300 1234 555
Cruelty Line 0300 1234 999
(24-hour service)
Web www.rspca.org.uk

The International Cat Association (TICA)

TICA is an international cat registry that runs shows throughout the UK.
Email regional.director.en@tica.org
Web www.tica-uk.org.uk

INDEX

Abyssinian 18
ageing 43, 94
aggression 104–105
air travel 75
allergies 5, 97
American Bobtail 18
American Curl 16
American Shorthair 18
American Wirehair 18
anxiety 106
appetite changes 62, 86
arthritis 86
asthma 86
attention-seeking 102

bad breath 86
balance 35
Balinese 16
behaviour 5, 100–107
behaviourists 107
Bengal 18
bereavement 95, 126
bi-coloured cats 13
Birman 16
birth 110–111
bites 96
bleeding 86
blindness 86
blue eyed cats, and deafness 14
body language 42
body shapes 9
Bombay 18
bones 30
brain 26–27
breathing problems 86
breeders 23
breeding 108–113
breeds 16–21
    characteristics 6
    showing cats 115
British Shorthair 10, 11, 18
broken bones 30
brushes 67
bullying 101
burial 95
Burmese 18–19
Burmilla 19
burns 87
bus travel 75
buying a cat 22–23

car travel 75
carriers 73–74
cartilage 30
cartoon cats 122
cat flap 50
cat flu 82, 87
cat scratch disease 96
catnip 52, 71
Cats Protection 22, 126
catteries 76, 77
cemeteries 95

Chantilly 17
character 6
Chartreux 11, 19
children 5, 46, 96
choosing a cat 6–15, 22–23
Christmas 51
claws 32
    clipping 68
    scratching 41, 53, 72, 104
climbing 72
coat 10
    colours 12
    fur 29
    grooming 67–69
    hairs 29, 40
    over-grooming 106
    patterns 13
    problems 67–68, 89
    texture 11
cobby body shape 9
collars 78
colourpoint cats 13
colours: coat 12
    eyes 14
    selective breeding 15
    sex-linked colours 14
    vision 37
communication 41–42
convulsions 87
Cornish Rex 19
costs of keeping a cat 4
coughing 87
cremation 95
curly-coated cats 11

deafness 14, 87
death 94–95
dementia 87
dental care 83
dependent cats 6, 102
Devon Rex 11, 19
diabetes mellitus 87–88
diarrhoea 88
diet see food
dogs 5, 8, 48, 54, 56
dribbling 88
drinking 39, 53, 60, 62, 63
drug therapy, behaviour
    problems 107

ears: cleaning 69
    deafness 14, 87
    hearing 34
    problems 88
eating: non-edible items 107
    see also food
Egyptian Mau 19
equipment: costs 4
    feeding cats 63
    showing cats 116
euthanasia 94
evolution 25

Exotic Shorthair 19
eyelid, third 38, 88
eyes: blindness 86
    cleaning 69
    colour 14
    problems 88
    sight 36–38

falls 35
famous cats 120–125
feeding cats 56–63
feline coronavirus (FCoV) 88
feline immunodeficiency
    virus (FIV) 88
feline infectious peritonitis
    (FIP) 88
feline leukaemia virus (FeLV)
    82, 88–89
feline lower urinary tract
    disease (FLUTD) 89
feline parvovirus (FPV) 82, 89
female cats (queens) 8, 81
fences 53
feral cats 6, 49
field of vision 38
finances 4
finding a cat 22–23, 79
fleas 54, 84, 96
food 56–63
    eating problems 61–62
    feeding a cat 56–60
    feeding equipment 63
    kittens 58, 60, 112, 113
    pregnant cats 58, 60, 109
foreign body shape 9
foreign travel 75
fur 29
    see also coat

games 71
gardens 52–55
GCCF Supreme Cat Show 118
ginger cats 14
gingivitis 88–89
glands 26–27, 28, 41
grass 50, 52
grooming 39, 67–69, 106
gum problems 88–89, 92

hairless cats 11
hairs 28–29
    colours 12
    hairballs 67
    whiskers 29, 40
    see also coat
handling cats 46
harnesses 55
head shapes 9
health: illnesses 86–93, 101
    kittens 112, 113
    owner's health 96–97
    preventative care 81–85

hearing 34
heart murmur 90
heat 109
high blood pressure 90
history 25
holidays 77
home: indoor cats 4, 49–51
    introducing a new cat 45, 48
    moving house 76
    outdoor cats 4, 52–55
homesitters 77
hormones 26, 27
hunting 6, 54–55
hyperthyroidism 90
hypoallergenic cats 97

identification 78
illness, kittens 113
illnesses see health
independent cats 6
indoor cats 4, 49–51
injuries 90
insurance 98–99
itching 90

Japanese Bobtail 19
joints 30
jumping 31, 72

kidney failure 91
kittens 7, 43
    birth 110–111
    buying 23
    coat 13
    food 58, 60, 112, 113
    raising 112–113
    vaccinations 82
Korat 20

labels, food 58
labour 110–111
lap cats 6
LaPerm 20
laws 119
legislation 119
lice 91
lifespan 43
lilies 51
limping 91
litter 64
litter trays 65, 66, 103
longhaired cats 10, 16–17
lost cats 54, 79

Maine Coon 16
male cats (toms) 8, 81
Manx 20
mating 109
matting, coat 67, 68
meat 56, 59
medicines 93
microchips 78

milk 60
milk fever 113
mites 88
moggies 15
mousers 6
mouth 39
  problems 86, 89–90
moving a cat 73–76
Munchkin 9, 20
muscles 28, 31

names 124
National Championship
  Shows 118
nerves 26–27, 28, 40
neutering 8, 81
night, eye sight 36
non-pedigree cats 15, 22
Norwegian Forest Cat 16
nose: cleaning 69
  problems 92
  sense of smell 33, 41

obesity 61, 62, 91
Ocicat 20
Oriental Longhair 10, 16
Oriental Shorthair 20
outdoor cats 4, 49, 52–55
over-grooming 106
overweight cats 61, 62

pain 27, 40
parasites 84–85, 97
patterns, coat 13
paws 32
pedigree cats 15, 22
Persian 6, 9, 10, 17
personality 6
Pet Passports 75
pets, introducing new cat to
  5, 47–48

PETS (Pet Travel Scheme) 75
petsitters 77, 126
pheromone therapy 107
pica 107
plants 51, 52, 54
play 70–71
pointed cats 13
poisons 51, 54, 91
polydactyl cats 32
pregnancy 60, 97, 109
preventative care 81–85
proverbs 121
pupils, eyes 37
purring 41

quarantine 75
queens (female cats) 8

rabies 75, 96
Ragdoll 17
reflective layer, eyes 37
rehoming cats 22
retina 37
ringworm 91–92, 96
roundworms 85, 97
rubbing 41
runs, outdoor 55
Russian Blue 20

safety 50–51, 54
salmonella 96
scent, communication 41
Scottish Fold 21
scratching 41, 53, 72, 104
security, lack of 101
self-coloured cats 12
Selkirk Rex 21
semi-longhaired cats 10
senses 33–40
settling a new cat 45–48
sex-linked colours 14

shaded hairs 12
shorthaired cats 10, 18–21
showing cats 114–118
Siamese 6, 9, 10, 15, 21
Siberian 17
sight 36–38
Singapura 21
sixth sense 33
skeleton 30
skin 28
sleep 70
smell, sense of 33, 41
smoke hairs 12
sneezing 92
Snowshoe 21
Somali 17
Sphynx 11, 21
spraying 41, 53, 102–103
stimulation, lack of 101
stings 92
stomatitis 89–90
straight-coated cats 11
sunburn 92
superstitions 123
swellings 92

tabby cats 13
'talking' 41
tapeworms 75, 85, 97
taste, sense of 39
teeth 39
  cleaning 69, 83
  problems 92
temperature sensitivity 40
territory marking 53, 72,
  102–103
texture, coat 11
therapies, behaviour
  problems 107
thirst 92
ticked hairs 12

ticks 54, 75, 92–93
Tiffany 17
tipped hairs 12
toes, extra 32
toileting 52, 64–66, 93, 103
tom cats 8
tongue 39
Tonkinese 21
tortoiseshell cats 13, 14
touch, sense of 40
toxoplasmosis 97
Toyger 9
toys 71
train travel 75
trauma 102
travel 73–75
trees 54
Turkish Angora 10, 17
Turkish Van 17
tuxedo cats 13

underweight cats 61, 62
urine, spraying 41, 53,
  102–103

vaccinations 82, 116
vets: and ageing cats 94
  insurance 98–99
  showing cats 117
vision 36–38
vomeronasal organ 33
vomiting 93

walking a cat 55
washing a cat 69
water: dislike of 29
  drinking 39, 53, 60, 62, 63
weight 61, 62
whiskers 29, 40
worms 54, 85, 97
wounds 86

ACKNOWLEDGEMENTS

Acknowledgement is made first and foremost to Susanna Wadeson at Transworld and to Dr. Hessayon, to Robin Watson for his illustrations, and to Brenda and Robert Updegraff, the editing and design duo. Thanks to the team at Transworld: Deborah Adams, Lisa Gordon, Manpreet Grewal, Sheila Lee, Alison Martin and Gareth Pottle, and to Hilary Bird for the index. Grateful acknowledgement is made to Gill Jackson and Angelina Gibbs for their painstaking proofreading, also to the GCCF, who helped unravel the complex world of showing, and to Cats Protection for their continuing good work neutering and rehoming cats across the UK. Finally, special thanks to Rebecca Watson's cat Bodmin and to Gill Jackson's cat Ellie, both of whom have provided endless hours of fun, companionship and inspiration.

Photographs
Alamy: 16 – middle left; 19 – top left; 115; 116 – all; 117 – bottom; 118 – bottom left; 122. **Bridgeman Archives:** 120. **Dr. D. G. Hessayon:** 128 – bottom left. **Drinkwell:** 63. **Hagen (UK):** 73 – bottom right. **Imperial War Museum:** 121. **iStock:** 11 – top right; 16 – top right; 18 – middle right; 20 – bottom right; 21 – middle right; 36 – bottom left, bottom right; 37 – bottom left, bottom right; 38 – bottom left, bottom middle; 39 – right; 44; 46 – bottom left; 54; 55 – top right; 56 – top middle; 61 – bottom right; 72 – middle left; 75 – bottom right; 79 – right; 95; 97 – all; 99; 101; 106 – all; 107; 117 – top right. **Press Association:** 125. **Rebecca Watson:** 67 – bottom right; 128 – bottom right. **Warren Photographic:** 1; 3; 5; 7 – all; 8; 10 – all; 11 – bottom; 14 – top left, middle right; 15 – all; 16 – bottom left; 17 – all; 18 – top left, top right, bottom right; 19 – middle right, bottom left; 20 – top left, top right; 21 – bottom left, bottom right; 22; 24; 29 – top right, bottom right; 32 – top right; 33 – middle right; 38 – bottom right; 40; 41 – all; 46 – middle right; 47; 49; 56 – bottom; 58 – bottom middle; 59 – top; 62; 65 – middle right; 66; 67 – top right; 70 – all; 71 – all; 73 – middle left; 74; 76; 78 – all; 80; 81; 82; 83 – all; 84 – top right; 85 – bottom right; 87; 88; 89 – all; 90; 91 – all; 92 – all; 93 – top right; 94; 96; 98; 100; 103 – bottom right; 104; 105 – top left; 108; 109 – all; 111 – bottom; 112; 113 – all; 114; 119.